CUMING'S TOUR TO THE WESTERN COUNTRY

(1807-1809) BY FORTESCUE CUMING

FORTESCUE CUMING

Made with ♥ on the Notion Press Platform
www.notionpress.com

Contents

CHAPTER ONE

What is Lorem Ipsum?
Lorem Ipsum is simply dummy text of the printing and typesetting industry. Lorem Ipsum has been the industry's standard dummy text ever since the 1500s, when an unknown printer took a galley of type and scrambled it to make a type specimen book. It has survived not only five centuries, but also the leap into electronic typesetting, remaining essentially unchanged. It was popularised in the 1960s with the release of Letraset sheets containing Lorem Ipsum passages, and more recently with desktop publishing software like Aldus PageMaker including versions of Lorem Ipsum.

Why do we use it?
It is a long established fact that a reader will be distracted by the readable content of a page when looking at its layout. The point of using Lorem Ipsum is that it has a more-or-less normal distribution of letters, as opposed to using 'Content here, content here', making it look like readable English. Many desktop publishing packages and web page editors now use Lorem Ipsum as their default model text, and a search for 'lorem ipsum' will uncover many web sites still in their infancy. Various versions have evolved over the years, sometimes by accident, sometimes on purpose (injected humour and the like).

Where does it come from?
Contrary to popular belief, Lorem Ipsum is not simply random text. It has roots in a piece of classical Latin literature from 45 BC, making it over 2000 years old. Richard McClintock, a Latin professor at Hampden-Sydney College in Virginia, looked up one of the more obscure Latin words, consectetur, from a Lorem Ipsum passage, and going through the cites of the word in classical literature, discovered the undoubtable source. Lorem Ipsum comes from sections 1.10.32 and 1.10.33 of "de Finibus Bonorum et Malorum" (The Extremes of Good and Evil) by Cicero, written in 45 BC. This book is a treatise on the theory of ethics, very popular during the Renaissance. The first line of Lorem Ipsum, "Lorem ipsum dolor sit amet..", comes from a line in section 1.10.32.

The standard chunk of Lorem Ipsum used since the 1500s is reproduced below for those interested. Sections 1.10.32 and 1.10.33 from "de Finibus Bonorum et Malorum" by Cicero are also reproduced in their exact original form, accompanied by English versions from the 1914 translation by H. Rackham.

Where can I get some?
There are many variations of passages of Lorem Ipsum available, but the majority have suffered alteration in some form, by injected humour, or randomised words which don't look even slightly believable. If you are going to use a passage of Lorem Ipsum, you need to be sure there isn't anything embarrassing hidden in the middle of text. All the Lorem Ipsum generators on the Internet tend to repeat predefined chunks as necessary, making this the first true generator on the Internet. It uses a dictionary of over 200 Latin words, combined with a handful of model sentence

structures, to generate Lorem Ipsum which looks reasonable. The generated Lorem Ipsum is therefore always free from repetition, injected humour, or non-characteristic words etc.

The standard Lorem Ipsum passage, used since the 1500s

"Lorem ipsum dolor sit amet, consectetur adipiscing elit, sed do eiusmod tempor incididunt ut labore et dolore magna aliqua. Ut enim ad minim veniam, quis nostrud exercitation ullamco laboris nisi ut aliquip ex ea commodo consequat. Duis aute irure dolor in reprehenderit in voluptate velit esse cillum dolore eu fugiat nulla pariatur. Excepteur sint occaecat cupidatat non proident, sunt in culpa qui officia deserunt mollit anim id est laborum."

Section 1.10.32 of "de Finibus Bonorum et Malorum", written by Cicero in 45 BC

"Sed ut perspiciatis unde omnis iste natus error sit voluptatem accusantium doloremque laudantium, totam rem aperiam, eaque ipsa quae ab illo inventore veritatis et quasi architecto beatae vitae dicta sunt explicabo. Nemo enim ipsam voluptatem quia voluptas sit aspernatur aut odit aut fugit, sed quia consequuntur magni dolores eos qui ratione voluptatem sequi nesciunt. Neque porro quisquam est, qui dolorem ipsum quia dolor sit amet, consectetur, adipisci velit, sed quia non numquam eius modi tempora incidunt ut labore et dolore magnam aliquam quaerat voluptatem. Ut enim ad minima veniam, quis nostrum exercitationem ullam corporis suscipit laboriosam, nisi ut aliquid ex ea commodi consequatur? Quis autem vel eum iure reprehenderit qui in ea voluptate velit esse quam nihil molestiae consequatur, vel illum qui dolorem eum fugiat quo voluptas nulla pariatur?"

1914 translation by H. Rackham

"But I must explain to you how all this mistaken idea of denouncing pleasure and praising pain was born and I will give you a complete account of the system, and expound the actual teachings of the great explorer of the truth, the master-builder of human happiness. No one rejects, dislikes, or avoids pleasure itself, because it is pleasure, but because those who do not know how to pursue pleasure rationally encounter consequences that are extremely painful. Nor again is there anyone who loves or pursues or desires to obtain pain of itself, because it is pain, but because occasionally circumstances occur in which toil and pain can procure him some great pleasure. To take a trivial example, which of us ever undertakes laborious physical exercise, except to obtain some advantage from it? But who has any right to find fault with a man who chooses to enjoy a pleasure that has no annoying consequences, or one who avoids a pain that produces no resultant pleasure?"

Section 1.10.33 of "de Finibus Bonorum et Malorum", written by Cicero in 45 BC

"At vero eos et accusamus et iusto odio dignissimos ducimus qui blanditiis praesentium voluptatum deleniti atque corrupti quos dolores et quas molestias excepturi sint occaecati cupiditate non provident, similique sunt in culpa qui officia deserunt mollitia animi, id est laborum et dolorum fuga. Et harum quidem rerum facilis est et expedita distinctio. Nam libero tempore, cum soluta nobis est eligendi optio cumque nihil impedit quo minus id quod maxime placeat facere possimus, omnis voluptas assumenda est, omnis dolor repellendus. Temporibus autem quibusdam et aut officiis debitis aut rerum necessitatibus saepe eveniet ut et voluptates repudiandae sint et molestiae non recusandae. Itaque earum rerum hic

tenetur a sapiente delectus, ut aut reiciendis voluptatibus maiores alias consequatur aut perferendis doloribus asperiores repellat."

1914 translation by H. Rackham

"On the other hand, we denounce with righteous indignation and dislike men who are so beguiled and demoralized by the charms of pleasure of the moment, so blinded by desire, that they cannot foresee the pain and trouble that are bound to ensue; and equal blame belongs to those who fail in their duty through weakness of will, which is the same as saying through shrinking from toil and pain. These cases are perfectly simple and easy to distinguish. In a free hour, when our power of choice is untrammelled and when nothing prevents our being able to do what we like best, every pleasure is to be welcomed and every pain avoided. But in certain circumstances and owing to the claims of duty or the obligations of business it will frequently occur that pleasures have to be repudiated and annoyances accepted. The wise man therefore always holds in these matters to this principle of selection: he rejects pleasures to secure other greater pleasures, or else he endures pains to avoid worse pains."

What is Lorem Ipsum?

Lorem Ipsum is simply dummy text of the printing and typesetting industry. Lorem Ipsum has been the industry's standard dummy text ever since the 1500s, when an unknown printer took a galley of type and scrambled it to make a type specimen book. It has survived not only five centuries, but also the leap into electronic typesetting, remaining essentially unchanged. It was popularised in the 1960s with the release of Letraset sheets containing Lorem Ipsum passages, and more recently with desktop publishing software like Aldus PageMaker including versions of Lorem

Ipsum.

Why do we use it?

It is a long established fact that a reader will be distracted by the readable content of a page when looking at its layout. The point of using Lorem Ipsum is that it has a more-or-less normal distribution of letters, as opposed to using 'Content here, content here', making it look like readable English. Many desktop publishing packages and web page editors now use Lorem Ipsum as their default model text, and a search for 'lorem ipsum' will uncover many web sites still in their infancy. Various versions have evolved over the years, sometimes by accident, sometimes on purpose (injected humour and the like).

Where does it come from?

Contrary to popular belief, Lorem Ipsum is not simply random text. It has roots in a piece of classical Latin literature from 45 BC, making it over 2000 years old. Richard McClintock, a Latin professor at Hampden-Sydney College in Virginia, looked up one of the more obscure Latin words, consectetur, from a Lorem Ipsum passage, and going through the cites of the word in classical literature, discovered the undoubtable source. Lorem Ipsum comes from sections 1.10.32 and 1.10.33 of "de Finibus Bonorum et Malorum" (The Extremes of Good and Evil) by Cicero, written in 45 BC. This book is a treatise on the theory of ethics, very popular during the Renaissance. The first line of Lorem Ipsum, "Lorem ipsum dolor sit amet..", comes from a line in section 1.10.32.

The standard chunk of Lorem Ipsum used since the 1500s is reproduced below for those interested. Sections 1.10.32 and 1.10.33 from "de Finibus Bonorum et Malorum" by Cicero are also reproduced in their exact

original form, accompanied by English versions from the 1914 translation by H. Rackham.

Where can I get some?

There are many variations of passages of Lorem Ipsum available, but the majority have suffered alteration in some form, by injected humour, or randomised words which don't look even slightly believable. If you are going to use a passage of Lorem Ipsum, you need to be sure there isn't anything embarrassing hidden in the middle of text. All the Lorem Ipsum generators on the Internet tend to repeat predefined chunks as necessary, making this the first true generator on the Internet. It uses a dictionary of over 200 Latin words, combined with a handful of model sentence structures, to generate Lorem Ipsum which looks reasonable. The generated Lorem Ipsum is therefore always free from repetition, injected humour, or non-characteristic words etc.

The standard Lorem Ipsum passage, used since the 1500s

"Lorem ipsum dolor sit amet, consectetur adipiscing elit, sed do eiusmod tempor incididunt ut labore et dolore magna aliqua. Ut enim ad minim veniam, quis nostrud exercitation ullamco laboris nisi ut aliquip ex ea commodo consequat. Duis aute irure dolor in reprehenderit in voluptate velit esse cillum dolore eu fugiat nulla pariatur. Excepteur sint occaecat cupidatat non proident, sunt in culpa qui officia deserunt mollit anim id est laborum."

Section 1.10.32 of "de Finibus Bonorum et Malorum", written by Cicero in 45 BC

"Sed ut perspiciatis unde omnis iste natus error sit voluptatem accusantium doloremque laudantium, totam rem aperiam, eaque ipsa quae ab illo inventore veritatis et quasi architecto beatae vitae dicta sunt explicabo. Nemo

enim ipsam voluptatem quia voluptas sit aspernatur aut odit aut fugit, sed quia consequuntur magni dolores eos qui ratione voluptatem sequi nesciunt. Neque porro quisquam est, qui dolorem ipsum quia dolor sit amet, consectetur, adipisci velit, sed quia non numquam eius modi tempora incidunt ut labore et dolore magnam aliquam quaerat voluptatem. Ut enim ad minima veniam, quis nostrum exercitationem ullam corporis suscipit laboriosam, nisi ut aliquid ex ea commodi consequatur? Quis autem vel eum iure reprehenderit qui in ea voluptate velit esse quam nihil molestiae consequatur, vel illum qui dolorem eum fugiat quo voluptas nulla pariatur?"

1914 translation by H. Rackham

"But I must explain to you how all this mistaken idea of denouncing pleasure and praising pain was born and I will give you a complete account of the system, and expound the actual teachings of the great explorer of the truth, the master-builder of human happiness. No one rejects, dislikes, or avoids pleasure itself, because it is pleasure, but because those who do not know how to pursue pleasure rationally encounter consequences that are extremely painful. Nor again is there anyone who loves or pursues or desires to obtain pain of itself, because it is pain, but because occasionally circumstances occur in which toil and pain can procure him some great pleasure. To take a trivial example, which of us ever undertakes laborious physical exercise, except to obtain some advantage from it? But who has any right to find fault with a man who chooses to enjoy a pleasure that has no annoying consequences, or one who avoids a pain that produces no resultant pleasure?"

Section 1.10.33 of "de Finibus Bonorum et Malorum", written by Cicero in 45 BC

"At vero eos et accusamus et iusto odio dignissimos

ducimus qui blanditiis praesentium voluptatum deleniti atque corrupti quos dolores et quas molestias excepturi sint occaecati cupiditate non provident, similique sunt in culpa qui officia deserunt mollitia animi, id est laborum et dolorum fuga. Et harum quidem rerum facilis est et expedita distinctio. Nam libero tempore, cum soluta nobis est eligendi optio cumque nihil impedit quo minus id quod maxime placeat facere possimus, omnis voluptas assumenda est, omnis dolor repellendus. Temporibus autem quibusdam et aut officiis debitis aut rerum necessitatibus saepe eveniet ut et voluptates repudiandae sint et molestiae non recusandae. Itaque earum rerum hic tenetur a sapiente delectus, ut aut reiciendis voluptatibus maiores alias consequatur aut perferendis doloribus asperiores repellat."

1914 translation by H. Rackham
"On the other hand, we denounce with righteous indignation and dislike men who are so beguiled and demoralized by the charms of pleasure of the moment, so blinded by desire, that they cannot foresee the pain and trouble that are bound to ensue; and equal blame belongs to those who fail in their duty through weakness of will, which is the same as saying through shrinking from toil and pain. These cases are perfectly simple and easy to distinguish. In a free hour, when our power of choice is untrammelled and when nothing prevents our being able to do what we like best, every pleasure is to be welcomed and every pain avoided. But in certain circumstances and owing to the claims of duty or the obligations of business it will frequently occur that pleasures have to be repudiated and annoyances accepted. The wise man therefore always holds in these matters to this principle of selection: he rejects pleasures to secure other greater pleasures, or else

he endures pains to avoid worse pains."

What is Lorem Ipsum?

Lorem Ipsum is simply dummy text of the printing and typesetting industry. Lorem Ipsum has been the industry's standard dummy text ever since the 1500s, when an unknown printer took a galley of type and scrambled it to make a type specimen book. It has survived not only five centuries, but also the leap into electronic typesetting, remaining essentially unchanged. It was popularised in the 1960s with the release of Letraset sheets containing Lorem Ipsum passages, and more recently with desktop publishing software like Aldus PageMaker including versions of Lorem Ipsum.

Why do we use it?

It is a long established fact that a reader will be distracted by the readable content of a page when looking at its layout. The point of using Lorem Ipsum is that it has a more-or-less normal distribution of letters, as opposed to using 'Content here, content here', making it look like readable English. Many desktop publishing packages and web page editors now use Lorem Ipsum as their default model text, and a search for 'lorem ipsum' will uncover many web sites still in their infancy. Various versions have evolved over the years, sometimes by accident, sometimes on purpose (injected humour and the like).

Where does it come from?

Contrary to popular belief, Lorem Ipsum is not simply random text. It has roots in a piece of classical Latin literature from 45 BC, making it over 2000 years old. Richard McClintock, a Latin professor at Hampden-Sydney College in Virginia, looked up one of the more obscure Latin words, consectetur, from a Lorem Ipsum passage, and going through the cites of the word in classical literature, discovered the undoubtable source. Lorem Ipsum comes from sections 1.10.32 and 1.10.33 of "de Finibus Bonorum et Malorum" (The Extremes of Good and Evil) by Cicero, written in 45 BC. This book is a treatise on the theory of ethics, very popular during the Renaissance. The first line of Lorem Ipsum, "Lorem ipsum dolor sit amet..", comes from a line in section 1.10.32.

The standard chunk of Lorem Ipsum used since the 1500s is reproduced below for those interested. Sections 1.10.32 and 1.10.33 from "de Finibus Bonorum et Malorum" by Cicero are also reproduced in their exact original form, accompanied by English versions from the 1914 translation by H. Rackham.

Where can I get some?

There are many variations of passages of Lorem Ipsum available, but the majority have suffered alteration in some form, by injected humour, or randomised words which don't look even slightly believable. If you are going to use a passage of Lorem Ipsum, you need to be sure there isn't anything embarrassing hidden in the middle of text. All the Lorem Ipsum generators on the Internet tend to repeat predefined chunks as necessary, making this the first true generator on the Internet. It uses a dictionary of over 200 Latin words, combined with a handful of model sentence structures, to generate Lorem Ipsum which looks reasonable. The generated Lorem Ipsum is therefore always free from repetition, injected humour, or non-characteristic words etc.

The standard Lorem Ipsum passage, used since the 1500s

"Lorem ipsum dolor sit amet, consectetur adipiscing elit, sed do eiusmod tempor incididunt ut labore et dolore magna aliqua. Ut enim ad minim veniam, quis nostrud exercitation ullamco laboris nisi ut aliquip ex ea commodo consequat. Duis aute irure dolor in reprehenderit in voluptate velit esse cillum dolore eu fugiat nulla pariatur. Excepteur sint occaecat cupidatat non proident, sunt in culpa qui officia deserunt mollit anim id est laborum."

Section 1.10.32 of "de Finibus Bonorum et Malorum", written by Cicero in 45 BC

"Sed ut perspiciatis unde omnis iste natus error sit voluptatem accusantium doloremque laudantium, totam rem aperiam, eaque ipsa quae ab illo inventore veritatis et quasi architecto beatae vitae dicta sunt explicabo. Nemo enim ipsam voluptatem quia voluptas sit aspernatur aut odit aut fugit, sed quia consequuntur magni dolores eos qui ratione voluptatem sequi nesciunt. Neque porro quisquam est, qui dolorem ipsum quia dolor sit amet, consectetur, adipisci velit, sed quia non numquam eius modi tempora incidunt ut labore et dolore magnam aliquam quaerat voluptatem. Ut enim ad minima veniam, quis nostrum exercitationem ullam corporis suscipit laboriosam, nisi ut aliquid ex ea commodi consequatur? Quis autem vel eum iure reprehenderit qui in ea voluptate velit esse quam nihil molestiae consequatur, vel illum qui dolorem eum fugiat quo voluptas nulla pariatur?"

1914 translation by H. Rackham

"But I must explain to you how all this mistaken idea of denouncing pleasure and praising pain was born and I will give you a complete account of the system, and expound the actual teachings of the great explorer of the truth, the master-builder of human happiness. No one rejects, dislikes, or avoids pleasure itself, because it is pleasure, but because those who do not know how to pursue pleasure rationally encounter consequences that are extremely painful. Nor again is there anyone who loves or pursues or desires to obtain pain of itself, because it is pain, but because occasionally circumstances occur in which toil and pain can procure him some great pleasure. To take a trivial example, which of us ever undertakes laborious physical exercise, except to obtain some advantage from it? But who has any right to find fault with a man who chooses to enjoy a pleasure that has no annoying consequences, or one who avoids a pain that produces no resultant pleasure?"

Section 1.10.33 of "de Finibus Bonorum et Malorum", written by Cicero in 45 BC

"At vero eos et accusamus et iusto odio dignissimos ducimus qui blanditiis praesentium voluptatum deleniti atque corrupti quos dolores et quas molestias excepturi sint occaecati cupiditate non provident, similique sunt in culpa qui officia deserunt mollitia animi, id est laborum et dolorum fuga. Et harum quidem rerum facilis est et expedita distinctio. Nam libero tempore, cum soluta nobis est eligendi optio cumque nihil impedit quo minus id quod maxime placeat facere possimus, omnis voluptas assumenda est, omnis dolor repellendus. Temporibus autem quibusdam et aut officiis debitis aut rerum necessitatibus saepe eveniet ut et voluptates repudiandae sint et molestiae non recusandae. Itaque earum rerum hic tenetur a sapiente delectus, ut aut reiciendis voluptatibus maiores alias consequatur aut perferendis doloribus asperiores repellat."

1914 translation by H. Rackham

"On the other hand, we denounce with righteous indignation and dislike men who are so beguiled and demoralized by the charms of pleasure of the moment, so blinded by desire, that they cannot foresee the pain and trouble that are bound to ensue; and equal blame belongs to those who fail in their duty through weakness of will, which is the same as saying through shrinking from toil and pain. These cases are perfectly simple and easy to distinguish. In a free hour, when our power of choice is untrammelled and when nothing prevents our being able to do what we like best, every pleasure is to be welcomed and every pain avoided. But in certain circumstances and owing to the claims of duty or the obligations of business it will frequently occur that pleasures have to be repudiated and annoyances accepted. The wise man therefore always holds in these matters to this principle of selection: he rejects pleasures to secure other greater pleasures, or else he endures pains to avoid worse pains."

What is Lorem Ipsum?

Lorem Ipsum is simply dummy text of the printing and typesetting industry. Lorem Ipsum has been the industry's standard dummy text ever since the 1500s, when an unknown printer took a galley of type and scrambled it to make a type specimen book. It has survived not only five centuries, but also the leap into electronic typesetting, remaining essentially unchanged. It was popularised in the 1960s with the release of Letraset sheets containing Lorem Ipsum passages, and more recently with desktop publishing software like Aldus PageMaker including versions of Lorem Ipsum.

Why do we use it?

It is a long established fact that a reader will be distracted by the readable content of a page when looking at its layout. The point of using Lorem Ipsum is that it has a more-or-less normal distribution of letters, as opposed to using 'Content here, content here', making it look like readable English. Many desktop publishing packages and web page editors now use Lorem Ipsum as their default model text, and a search for 'lorem ipsum' will uncover many web sites still in their infancy. Various versions have evolved over the years, sometimes by accident, sometimes on purpose (injected humour and the like).

Where does it come from?
Contrary to popular belief, Lorem Ipsum is not simply random text. It has roots in a piece of classical Latin literature from 45 BC, making it over 2000 years old. Richard McClintock, a Latin professor at Hampden-Sydney College in Virginia, looked up one of the more obscure Latin words, consectetur, from a Lorem Ipsum passage, and going through the cites of the word in classical literature, discovered the undoubtable source. Lorem Ipsum comes from sections 1.10.32 and 1.10.33 of "de Finibus Bonorum et Malorum" (The Extremes of Good and Evil) by Cicero, written in 45 BC. This book is a treatise on the theory of ethics, very popular during the Renaissance. The first line of Lorem Ipsum, "Lorem ipsum dolor sit amet..", comes from a line in section 1.10.32.

The standard chunk of Lorem Ipsum used since the 1500s is reproduced below for those interested. Sections 1.10.32 and 1.10.33 from "de Finibus Bonorum et Malorum" by Cicero are also reproduced in their exact original form, accompanied by English versions from the 1914 translation by H. Rackham.

Where can I get some?
There are many variations of passages of Lorem Ipsum available, but the majority have suffered alteration in some form, by injected humour, or randomised words which don't look even slightly believable. If you are going to use a passage of Lorem Ipsum, you need to be sure there isn't anything embarrassing hidden in the middle of text. All

the Lorem Ipsum generators on the Internet tend to repeat predefined chunks as necessary, making this the first true generator on the Internet. It uses a dictionary of over 200 Latin words, combined with a handful of model sentence structures, to generate Lorem Ipsum which looks reasonable. The generated Lorem Ipsum is therefore always free from repetition, injected humour, or non-characteristic words etc.

The standard Lorem Ipsum passage, used since the 1500s

"Lorem ipsum dolor sit amet, consectetur adipiscing elit, sed do eiusmod tempor incididunt ut labore et dolore magna aliqua. Ut enim ad minim veniam, quis nostrud exercitation ullamco laboris nisi ut aliquip ex ea commodo consequat. Duis aute irure dolor in reprehenderit in voluptate velit esse cillum dolore eu fugiat nulla pariatur. Excepteur sint occaecat cupidatat non proident, sunt in culpa qui officia deserunt mollit anim id est laborum."

Section 1.10.32 of "de Finibus Bonorum et Malorum", written by Cicero in 45 BC

"Sed ut perspiciatis unde omnis iste natus error sit voluptatem accusantium doloremque laudantium, totam rem aperiam, eaque ipsa quae ab illo inventore veritatis et quasi architecto beatae vitae dicta sunt explicabo. Nemo enim ipsam voluptatem quia voluptas sit aspernatur aut odit aut fugit, sed quia consequuntur magni dolores eos qui ratione voluptatem sequi nesciunt. Neque porro quisquam est, qui dolorem ipsum quia dolor sit amet, consectetur, adipisci velit, sed quia non numquam eius modi tempora incidunt ut labore et dolore magnam aliquam quaerat voluptatem. Ut enim ad minima veniam, quis nostrum exercitationem ullam corporis suscipit laboriosam, nisi ut aliquid ex ea commodi consequatur? Quis autem vel eum iure reprehenderit qui in ea voluptate velit esse quam nihil molestiae consequatur, vel illum qui dolorem eum fugiat quo voluptas nulla pariatur?"

1914 translation by H. Rackham

"But I must explain to you how all this mistaken idea of denouncing pleasure and praising pain was born and I will give you a complete account of the system, and expound the actual teachings of the great explorer of the truth, the master-builder of human happiness. No one rejects, dislikes, or avoids pleasure itself, because it is pleasure, but because those who do not know how to pursue pleasure rationally encounter consequences that are extremely painful. Nor again is there anyone who loves or pursues or desires to obtain pain of itself, because it is pain, but because occasionally circumstances occur in which toil and pain can procure him some great pleasure. To take a trivial example, which of us ever undertakes laborious physical exercise, except to obtain some advantage from it? But who has any right to find fault with a man who chooses to enjoy a pleasure that has no annoying consequences, or one who avoids a pain that produces no resultant pleasure?"

Section 1.10.33 of "de Finibus Bonorum et Malorum", written by Cicero in 45 BC

"At vero eos et accusamus et iusto odio dignissimos ducimus qui blanditiis praesentium voluptatum deleniti atque corrupti quos dolores et quas molestias excepturi sint occaecati cupiditate non provident, similique sunt in culpa qui officia deserunt mollitia animi, id est laborum et dolorum fuga. Et harum quidem rerum facilis est et expedita distinctio. Nam libero tempore, cum soluta nobis est eligendi optio cumque nihil impedit quo minus id quod maxime placeat facere possimus, omnis voluptas assumenda est, omnis dolor repellendus. Temporibus autem quibusdam et aut officiis debitis aut rerum necessitatibus saepe eveniet ut et voluptates repudiandae sint et molestiae non recusandae. Itaque earum rerum hic tenetur a sapiente delectus, ut aut reiciendis voluptatibus maiores alias consequatur aut perferendis doloribus asperiores repellat."

1914 translation by H. Rackham

"On the other hand, we denounce with righteous indignation and dislike men who are so beguiled and demoralized by the charms of pleasure of the moment, so blinded by desire, that they cannot foresee the pain and trouble that are bound to ensue; and equal blame belongs to those who fail in their duty through weakness of will, which is the same as saying through shrinking from toil and pain. These cases are perfectly simple and easy to distinguish. In a free hour, when our power of choice is untrammelled and when nothing prevents our being able to do what we like best, every pleasure is to be welcomed and every pain avoided. But in certain circumstances and owing to the claims of duty or the obligations of business it will frequently occur that pleasures have to be repudiated and annoyances accepted. The wise man therefore always holds in these matters to this principle of selection: he rejects pleasures to secure other greater pleasures, or else he endures pains to avoid worse pains."

What is Lorem Ipsum?

Lorem Ipsum is simply dummy text of the printing and typesetting industry. Lorem Ipsum has been the industry's standard dummy text ever since the 1500s, when an unknown printer took a galley of type and scrambled it to make a type specimen book. It has survived not only five centuries, but also the leap into electronic typesetting, remaining essentially unchanged. It was popularised in the

1960s with the release of Letraset sheets containing Lorem Ipsum passages, and more recently with desktop publishing software like Aldus PageMaker including versions of Lorem Ipsum.

Why do we use it?

It is a long established fact that a reader will be distracted by the readable content of a page when looking at its layout. The point of using Lorem Ipsum is that it has a more-or-less normal distribution of letters, as opposed to using 'Content here, content here', making it look like readable English. Many desktop publishing packages and web page editors now use Lorem Ipsum as their default model text, and a search for 'lorem ipsum' will uncover many web sites still in their infancy. Various versions have evolved over the years, sometimes by accident, sometimes on purpose (injected humour and the like).

Where does it come from?

Contrary to popular belief, Lorem Ipsum is not simply random text. It has roots in a piece of classical Latin literature from 45 BC, making it over 2000 years old. Richard McClintock, a Latin professor at Hampden-Sydney College in Virginia, looked up one of the more obscure Latin words, consectetur, from a Lorem Ipsum passage, and going through the cites of the word in classical literature, discovered the undoubtable source. Lorem Ipsum comes from sections 1.10.32 and 1.10.33 of "de Finibus Bonorum et Malorum" (The Extremes of Good and Evil) by Cicero, written in 45 BC. This book is a treatise on the theory of ethics, very popular during the Renaissance. The first line of Lorem Ipsum, "Lorem ipsum dolor sit amet..", comes from a line in section 1.10.32.

The standard chunk of Lorem Ipsum used since the 1500s is reproduced below for those interested. Sections 1.10.32 and 1.10.33 from "de Finibus Bonorum et Malorum" by Cicero are also reproduced in their exact original form, accompanied by English versions from the 1914 translation by H. Rackham.

Where can I get some?

There are many variations of passages of Lorem Ipsum available, but the majority have suffered alteration in some form, by injected humour, or randomised words which don't look even slightly believable. If you are going to use a passage of Lorem Ipsum, you need to be sure there isn't anything embarrassing hidden in the middle of text. All the Lorem Ipsum generators on the Internet tend to repeat predefined chunks as necessary, making this the first true generator on the Internet. It uses a dictionary of over 200 Latin words, combined with a handful of model sentence structures, to generate Lorem Ipsum which looks reasonable. The generated Lorem Ipsum is therefore always free from repetition, injected humour, or non-characteristic words etc.

The standard Lorem Ipsum passage, used since the 1500s

"Lorem ipsum dolor sit amet, consectetur adipiscing elit, sed do eiusmod tempor incididunt ut labore et dolore magna aliqua. Ut enim ad minim veniam, quis nostrud exercitation ullamco laboris nisi ut aliquip ex ea commodo consequat. Duis aute irure dolor in reprehenderit in voluptate velit esse cillum dolore eu fugiat nulla pariatur. Excepteur sint occaecat cupidatat non proident, sunt in culpa qui officia deserunt mollit anim id est laborum."

Section 1.10.32 of "de Finibus Bonorum et Malorum", written by Cicero in 45 BC

"Sed ut perspiciatis unde omnis iste natus error sit voluptatem accusantium doloremque laudantium, totam rem aperiam, eaque ipsa quae ab illo inventore veritatis et quasi architecto beatae vitae dicta sunt explicabo. Nemo enim ipsam voluptatem quia voluptas sit aspernatur aut odit aut fugit, sed quia consequuntur magni dolores eos qui ratione voluptatem sequi nesciunt. Neque porro quisquam est, qui dolorem ipsum quia dolor sit amet, consectetur, adipisci velit, sed quia non numquam eius modi tempora incidunt ut labore et dolore magnam aliquam quaerat voluptatem. Ut enim ad minima veniam, quis nostrum exercitationem ullam corporis suscipit laboriosam, nisi ut aliquid ex ea commodi consequatur? Quis autem vel eum iure reprehenderit qui in ea voluptate velit esse quam nihil molestiae consequatur, vel illum qui dolorem eum fugiat quo voluptas nulla pariatur?"

1914 translation by H. Rackham

"But I must explain to you how all this mistaken idea of denouncing pleasure and praising pain was born and I will give you a complete account of the system, and expound the actual teachings of the great explorer of the truth, the master-builder of human happiness. No one rejects, dislikes, or avoids pleasure itself, because it is pleasure, but because those who do not know how to pursue pleasure rationally encounter consequences that are extremely painful. Nor again is there anyone who loves or pursues or desires to obtain pain of itself, because it is pain, but because occasionally circumstances occur in which toil and pain can procure him some great pleasure. To take a trivial example, which of us ever undertakes laborious physical exercise, except to obtain some advantage from it? But who has any right to find fault with a man who chooses to enjoy a pleasure that has no annoying consequences, or one who avoids a pain that produces no resultant pleasure?"

Section 1.10.33 of "de Finibus Bonorum et Malorum", written by Cicero in 45 BC

"At vero eos et accusamus et iusto odio dignissimos ducimus qui blanditiis praesentium voluptatum deleniti atque corrupti quos dolores et quas molestias excepturi sint occaecati cupiditate non provident, similique sunt in culpa qui officia deserunt mollitia animi, id est laborum et dolorum fuga. Et harum quidem rerum facilis est et expedita distinctio. Nam libero tempore, cum soluta nobis est eligendi optio cumque nihil impedit quo minus id quod maxime placeat facere possimus, omnis voluptas assumenda est, omnis dolor repellendus. Temporibus autem quibusdam et aut officiis debitis aut rerum necessitatibus saepe eveniet ut et voluptates repudiandae sint et molestiae non recusandae. Itaque earum rerum hic tenetur a sapiente delectus, ut aut reiciendis voluptatibus maiores alias consequatur aut perferendis doloribus asperiores repellat."

1914 translation by H. Rackham

"On the other hand, we denounce with righteous indignation and dislike men who are so beguiled and demoralized by the charms of pleasure of the moment, so blinded by desire, that they cannot foresee the pain and trouble that are bound to ensue; and equal blame belongs to those who fail in their duty through weakness of will, which is the same as saying through shrinking from toil and pain. These cases are perfectly simple and easy to distinguish. In a free hour, when our power of choice is untrammelled and when nothing prevents our being able to do what we like best, every pleasure is to be welcomed and every pain avoided. But in certain circumstances and owing to the claims of duty or the obligations of business it will frequently occur that pleasures have to be repudiated and annoyances accepted. The wise man therefore always holds in these matters to this principle of selection: he rejects pleasures to secure other greater pleasures, or else he endures pains to avoid worse pains."

What is Lorem Ipsum?

Lorem Ipsum is simply dummy text of the printing and typesetting industry. Lorem Ipsum has been the industry's standard dummy text ever since the 1500s, when an unknown printer took a galley of type and scrambled it to make a type specimen book. It has survived not only five centuries, but also the leap into electronic typesetting, remaining essentially unchanged. It was popularised in the 1960s with the release of Letraset sheets containing Lorem Ipsum passages, and more recently with desktop publishing software like Aldus PageMaker including versions of Lorem Ipsum.

Why do we use it?

It is a long established fact that a reader will be distracted by the readable content of a page when looking at its layout. The point of using Lorem Ipsum is that it has a more-or-less normal distribution of letters, as opposed to using 'Content here, content here', making it look like readable English. Many desktop publishing packages and web page editors now use Lorem Ipsum as their default model text, and a search for 'lorem ipsum' will uncover many web sites still in their infancy. Various versions have evolved over the years, sometimes by accident, sometimes on purpose (injected humour and the like).

Where does it come from?

Contrary to popular belief, Lorem Ipsum is not simply random text. It has roots in a piece of classical Latin literature from 45 BC, making it over 2000 years old. Richard McClintock, a Latin professor at Hampden-Sydney College in Virginia, looked up one of the more obscure Latin words, consectetur, from a Lorem Ipsum passage, and going through the cites of the word in classical literature, discovered the undoubtable source. Lorem Ipsum comes from sections 1.10.32 and 1.10.33 of "de Finibus Bonorum et Malorum" (The Extremes of Good and Evil) by Cicero, written in 45 BC. This book is a treatise on the theory of ethics, very popular during the Renaissance. The first line of Lorem Ipsum, "Lorem ipsum dolor sit amet..", comes from a line in section 1.10.32.

The standard chunk of Lorem Ipsum used since the 1500s is reproduced below for those interested. Sections 1.10.32 and 1.10.33 from "de Finibus Bonorum et Malorum" by Cicero are also reproduced in their exact original form, accompanied by English versions from the 1914 translation by H. Rackham.

Where can I get some?

There are many variations of passages of Lorem Ipsum available, but the majority have suffered alteration in some form, by injected humour, or randomised words which don't look even slightly believable. If you are going to use a passage of Lorem Ipsum, you need to be sure there isn't anything embarrassing hidden in the middle of text. All the Lorem Ipsum generators on the Internet tend to repeat predefined chunks as necessary, making this the first true generator on the Internet. It uses a dictionary of over 200 Latin words, combined with a handful of model sentence structures, to generate Lorem Ipsum which looks reasonable. The generated Lorem Ipsum is therefore always free from repetition, injected humour, or non-characteristic words etc.

The standard Lorem Ipsum passage, used since the 1500s

"Lorem ipsum dolor sit amet, consectetur adipiscing elit, sed do eiusmod tempor incididunt ut labore et dolore magna aliqua. Ut enim ad minim veniam, quis nostrud exercitation ullamco laboris nisi ut aliquip ex ea commodo consequat. Duis aute irure dolor in reprehenderit in voluptate velit esse cillum dolore eu fugiat nulla pariatur. Excepteur sint occaecat cupidatat non proident, sunt in culpa qui officia deserunt mollit anim id est laborum."

Section 1.10.32 of "de Finibus Bonorum et Malorum", written by Cicero in 45 BC

"Sed ut perspiciatis unde omnis iste natus error sit voluptatem accusantium doloremque laudantium, totam rem aperiam, eaque ipsa quae ab illo inventore veritatis et quasi architecto beatae vitae dicta sunt explicabo. Nemo enim ipsam voluptatem quia voluptas sit aspernatur aut odit aut fugit, sed quia consequuntur magni dolores eos qui ratione voluptatem sequi nesciunt. Neque porro quisquam est, qui dolorem ipsum quia dolor sit amet, consectetur, adipisci velit, sed quia non numquam eius modi tempora incidunt ut labore et dolore magnam aliquam quaerat voluptatem. Ut enim ad minima veniam, quis nostrum exercitationem ullam corporis suscipit laboriosam, nisi ut aliquid ex ea commodi consequatur? Quis autem vel eum iure reprehenderit qui in ea voluptate velit esse quam nihil molestiae consequatur, vel illum qui dolorem eum fugiat quo voluptas nulla pariatur?"

1914 translation by H. Rackham

"But I must explain to you how all this mistaken idea of denouncing pleasure and praising pain was born and I will give you a complete account of the system, and expound the actual teachings of the great explorer of the truth, the master-builder of human happiness. No one rejects, dislikes, or avoids pleasure itself, because it is pleasure, but because those who do not know how to pursue pleasure rationally encounter consequences that are extremely painful. Nor again is there anyone who loves or pursues or desires to obtain pain of itself, because it is pain, but because occasionally circumstances occur in which toil and pain can procure him some great pleasure. To take a trivial example, which of us ever undertakes laborious physical exercise, except to obtain some advantage from it? But who has any right to find fault with a man who chooses to enjoy a pleasure that has no annoying consequences, or one who avoids a pain that produces no resultant pleasure?"

Section 1.10.33 of "de Finibus Bonorum et Malorum", written by Cicero in 45 BC

"At vero eos et accusamus et iusto odio dignissimos ducimus qui blanditiis praesentium voluptatum deleniti atque corrupti quos dolores et quas molestias excepturi sint occaecati cupiditate non provident, similique sunt in culpa qui officia deserunt mollitia animi, id est laborum et dolorum fuga. Et harum quidem rerum facilis est et expedita distinctio. Nam libero tempore, cum soluta nobis est eligendi optio cumque nihil impedit quo minus id quod maxime placeat facere possimus, omnis voluptas assumenda est, omnis dolor repellendus. Temporibus autem quibusdam et aut officiis debitis aut rerum necessitatibus saepe eveniet ut et voluptates repudiandae sint et molestiae non recusandae. Itaque earum rerum hic tenetur a sapiente delectus, ut aut reiciendis voluptatibus maiores alias consequatur aut perferendis doloribus asperiores repellat."

1914 translation by H. Rackham

"On the other hand, we denounce with righteous

indignation and dislike men who are so beguiled and demoralized by the charms of pleasure of the moment, so blinded by desire, that they cannot foresee the pain and trouble that are bound to ensue; and equal blame belongs to those who fail in their duty through weakness of will, which is the same as saying through shrinking from toil and pain. These cases are perfectly simple and easy to distinguish. In a free hour, when our power of choice is untrammelled and when nothing prevents our being able to do what we like best, every pleasure is to be welcomed and every pain avoided. But in certain circumstances and owing to the claims of duty or the obligations of business it will frequently occur that pleasures have to be repudiated and annoyances accepted. The wise man therefore always holds in these matters to this principle of selection: he rejects pleasures to secure other greater pleasures, or else he endures pains to avoid worse pains."

What is Lorem Ipsum?

Lorem Ipsum is simply dummy text of the printing and typesetting industry. Lorem Ipsum has been the industry's standard dummy text ever since the 1500s, when an unknown printer took a galley of type and scrambled it to make a type specimen book. It has survived not only five centuries, but also the leap into electronic typesetting, remaining essentially unchanged. It was popularised in the 1960s with the release of Letraset sheets containing Lorem Ipsum passages, and more recently with desktop publishing software like Aldus PageMaker including versions of Lorem Ipsum.

Why do we use it?

It is a long established fact that a reader will be distracted by the readable content of a page when looking at its layout. The point of using Lorem Ipsum is that it has a more-or-less normal distribution of letters, as opposed to using 'Content here, content here', making it look like readable English. Many desktop publishing packages and web page editors now use Lorem Ipsum as their default model text, and a search for 'lorem ipsum' will uncover many web sites still in their infancy. Various versions have evolved over the years, sometimes by accident, sometimes on purpose (injected humour and the like).

Where does it come from?
Contrary to popular belief, Lorem Ipsum is not simply random text. It has roots in a piece of classical Latin literature from 45 BC, making it over 2000 years old. Richard McClintock, a Latin professor at Hampden-Sydney College in Virginia, looked up one of the more obscure Latin words, consectetur, from a Lorem Ipsum passage, and going through the cites of the word in classical literature, discovered the undoubtable source. Lorem Ipsum comes from sections 1.10.32 and 1.10.33 of "de Finibus Bonorum et Malorum" (The Extremes of Good and Evil) by Cicero, written in 45 BC. This book is a treatise on the theory of ethics, very popular during the Renaissance. The first line of Lorem Ipsum, "Lorem ipsum dolor sit amet..", comes from a line in section 1.10.32.

The standard chunk of Lorem Ipsum used since the 1500s is reproduced below for those interested. Sections 1.10.32 and 1.10.33 from "de Finibus Bonorum et Malorum" by Cicero are also reproduced in their exact original form, accompanied by English versions from the 1914 translation by H. Rackham.

Where can I get some?
There are many variations of passages of Lorem Ipsum available, but the majority have suffered alteration in some

form, by injected humour, or randomised words which don't look even slightly believable. If you are going to use a passage of Lorem Ipsum, you need to be sure there isn't anything embarrassing hidden in the middle of text. All the Lorem Ipsum generators on the Internet tend to repeat predefined chunks as necessary, making this the first true generator on the Internet. It uses a dictionary of over 200 Latin words, combined with a handful of model sentence structures, to generate Lorem Ipsum which looks reasonable. The generated Lorem Ipsum is therefore always free from repetition, injected humour, or non-characteristic words etc.

The standard Lorem Ipsum passage, used since the 1500s

"Lorem ipsum dolor sit amet, consectetur adipiscing elit, sed do eiusmod tempor incididunt ut labore et dolore magna aliqua. Ut enim ad minim veniam, quis nostrud exercitation ullamco laboris nisi ut aliquip ex ea commodo consequat. Duis aute irure dolor in reprehenderit in voluptate velit esse cillum dolore eu fugiat nulla pariatur. Excepteur sint occaecat cupidatat non proident, sunt in culpa qui officia deserunt mollit anim id est laborum."

Section 1.10.32 of "de Finibus Bonorum et Malorum", written by Cicero in 45 BC

"Sed ut perspiciatis unde omnis iste natus error sit voluptatem accusantium doloremque laudantium, totam rem aperiam, eaque ipsa quae ab illo inventore veritatis et quasi architecto beatae vitae dicta sunt explicabo. Nemo enim ipsam voluptatem quia voluptas sit aspernatur aut odit aut fugit, sed quia consequuntur magni dolores eos qui ratione voluptatem sequi nesciunt. Neque porro quisquam est, qui dolorem ipsum quia dolor sit amet, consectetur, adipisci velit, sed quia non numquam eius modi tempora incidunt ut labore et dolore magnam aliquam quaerat voluptatem. Ut enim ad minima veniam, quis nostrum exercitationem ullam corporis suscipit laboriosam, nisi ut aliquid ex ea commodi consequatur? Quis autem vel eum iure reprehenderit qui in ea voluptate velit esse quam nihil molestiae consequatur, vel illum qui dolorem eum fugiat quo voluptas nulla pariatur?"

1914 translation by H. Rackham

"But I must explain to you how all this mistaken idea of denouncing pleasure and praising pain was born and I will give you a complete account of the system, and expound the actual teachings of the great explorer of the truth, the master-builder of human happiness. No one rejects, dislikes, or avoids pleasure itself, because it is pleasure, but because those who do not know how to pursue pleasure rationally encounter consequences that are extremely painful. Nor again is there anyone who loves or pursues or desires to obtain pain of itself, because it is pain, but because occasionally circumstances occur in which toil and pain can procure him some great pleasure. To take a trivial example, which of us ever undertakes laborious physical exercise, except to obtain some advantage from it? But who has any right to find fault with a man who chooses to enjoy a pleasure that has no annoying consequences, or one who avoids a pain that produces no resultant pleasure?"

Section 1.10.33 of "de Finibus Bonorum et Malorum", written by Cicero in 45 BC

"At vero eos et accusamus et iusto odio dignissimos ducimus qui blanditiis praesentium voluptatum deleniti atque corrupti quos dolores et quas molestias excepturi sint occaecati cupiditate non provident, similique sunt in culpa qui officia deserunt mollitia animi, id est laborum et dolorum fuga. Et harum quidem rerum facilis est et expedita distinctio. Nam libero tempore, cum soluta nobis est eligendi optio cumque nihil impedit quo minus id quod maxime placeat facere possimus, omnis voluptas assumenda est, omnis dolor repellendus. Temporibus autem quibusdam et aut officiis debitis aut rerum necessitatibus saepe eveniet ut et voluptates repudiandae sint et molestiae non recusandae. Itaque earum rerum hic tenetur a sapiente delectus, ut aut reiciendis voluptatibus maiores alias consequatur aut perferendis doloribus asperiores repellat."

1914 translation by H. Rackham

"On the other hand, we denounce with righteous indignation and dislike men who are so beguiled and demoralized by the charms of pleasure of the moment, so blinded by desire, that they cannot foresee the pain and trouble that are bound to ensue; and equal blame belongs to those who fail in their duty through weakness of will, which is the same as saying through shrinking from toil and pain. These cases are perfectly simple and easy to distinguish. In a free hour, when our power of choice is untrammelled and when nothing prevents our being able to do what we like best, every pleasure is to be welcomed and every pain avoided. But in certain circumstances and owing to the claims of duty or the obligations of business it will frequently occur that pleasures have to be repudiated and annoyances accepted. The wise man therefore always holds in these matters to this principle of selection: he rejects pleasures to secure other greater pleasures, or else he endures pains to avoid worse pains."

What is Lorem Ipsum?

Lorem Ipsum is simply dummy text of the printing and typesetting industry. Lorem Ipsum has been the industry's standard dummy text ever since the 1500s, when an unknown printer took a galley of type and scrambled it to make a type specimen book. It has survived not only five centuries, but also the leap into electronic typesetting, remaining essentially unchanged. It was popularised in the 1960s with the release of Letraset sheets containing Lorem Ipsum passages, and more recently with desktop publishing software like Aldus PageMaker including versions of Lorem Ipsum.

Why do we use it?

It is a long established fact that a reader will be distracted by the readable content of a page when looking at its layout. The point of using Lorem Ipsum is that it has a more-or-less normal distribution of letters, as opposed to using 'Content here, content here', making it look like readable English. Many desktop publishing packages and web page editors now use Lorem Ipsum as their default model text, and a search for 'lorem ipsum' will uncover many web sites still in their infancy. Various versions have evolved over the years, sometimes by accident, sometimes on purpose (injected humour and the like).

Where does it come from?

Contrary to popular belief, Lorem Ipsum is not simply random text. It has roots in a piece of classical Latin literature from 45 BC, making it over 2000 years old. Richard McClintock, a Latin professor at Hampden-Sydney College in Virginia, looked up one of the more obscure Latin words, consectetur, from a Lorem Ipsum passage, and going through the cites of the word in classical literature, discovered the undoubtable source. Lorem Ipsum comes from sections 1.10.32 and 1.10.33 of "de Finibus Bonorum et Malorum" (The Extremes of Good and Evil) by Cicero, written in 45 BC. This book is a treatise on the theory of ethics, very popular during the Renaissance. The first line of Lorem Ipsum, "Lorem ipsum dolor sit amet..", comes from a line in section 1.10.32.

The standard chunk of Lorem Ipsum used since the 1500s is reproduced below for those interested. Sections 1.10.32 and 1.10.33 from "de Finibus Bonorum et Malorum" by Cicero are also reproduced in their exact original form, accompanied by English versions from the 1914 translation by H. Rackham.

Where can I get some?
There are many variations of passages of Lorem Ipsum available, but the majority have suffered alteration in some form, by injected humour, or randomised words which don't look even slightly believable. If you are going to use a passage of Lorem Ipsum, you need to be sure there isn't anything embarrassing hidden in the middle of text. All the Lorem Ipsum generators on the Internet tend to repeat predefined chunks as necessary, making this the first true generator on the Internet. It uses a dictionary of over 200 Latin words, combined with a handful of model sentence structures, to generate Lorem Ipsum which looks reasonable. The generated Lorem Ipsum is therefore always free from repetition, injected humour, or non-characteristic words etc.

The standard Lorem Ipsum passage, used since the 1500s
"Lorem ipsum dolor sit amet, consectetur adipiscing elit, sed do eiusmod tempor incididunt ut labore et dolore magna aliqua. Ut enim ad minim veniam, quis nostrud exercitation ullamco laboris nisi ut aliquip ex ea commodo consequat. Duis aute irure dolor in reprehenderit in voluptate velit esse cillum dolore eu fugiat nulla pariatur. Excepteur sint occaecat cupidatat non proident, sunt in

culpa qui officia deserunt mollit anim id est laborum."

Section 1.10.32 of "de Finibus Bonorum et Malorum", written by Cicero in 45 BC

"Sed ut perspiciatis unde omnis iste natus error sit voluptatem accusantium doloremque laudantium, totam rem aperiam, eaque ipsa quae ab illo inventore veritatis et quasi architecto beatae vitae dicta sunt explicabo. Nemo enim ipsam voluptatem quia voluptas sit aspernatur aut odit aut fugit, sed quia consequuntur magni dolores eos qui ratione voluptatem sequi nesciunt. Neque porro quisquam est, qui dolorem ipsum quia dolor sit amet, consectetur, adipisci velit, sed quia non numquam eius modi tempora incidunt ut labore et dolore magnam aliquam quaerat voluptatem. Ut enim ad minima veniam, quis nostrum exercitationem ullam corporis suscipit laboriosam, nisi ut aliquid ex ea commodi consequatur? Quis autem vel eum iure reprehenderit qui in ea voluptate velit esse quam nihil molestiae consequatur, vel illum qui dolorem eum fugiat quo voluptas nulla pariatur?"

1914 translation by H. Rackham

"But I must explain to you how all this mistaken idea of denouncing pleasure and praising pain was born and I will give you a complete account of the system, and expound the actual teachings of the great explorer of the truth, the master-builder of human happiness. No one rejects, dislikes, or avoids pleasure itself, because it is pleasure, but because those who do not know how to pursue pleasure rationally encounter consequences that are extremely painful. Nor again is there anyone who loves or pursues or desires to obtain pain of itself, because it is pain, but because occasionally circumstances occur in which toil and pain can procure him some great pleasure. To take a trivial example, which of us ever undertakes laborious physical exercise, except to obtain some advantage from it? But who has any right to find fault with a man who chooses to enjoy a pleasure that has no annoying consequences, or one who avoids a pain that produces no resultant pleasure?"

Section 1.10.33 of "de Finibus Bonorum et Malorum", written by Cicero in 45 BC

"At vero eos et accusamus et iusto odio dignissimos ducimus qui blanditiis praesentium voluptatum deleniti atque corrupti quos dolores et quas molestias excepturi sint occaecati cupiditate non provident, similique sunt in culpa qui officia deserunt mollitia animi, id est laborum et dolorum fuga. Et harum quidem rerum facilis est et expedita distinctio. Nam libero tempore, cum soluta nobis est eligendi optio cumque nihil impedit quo minus id quod maxime placeat facere possimus, omnis voluptas assumenda est, omnis dolor repellendus. Temporibus autem quibusdam et aut officiis debitis aut rerum necessitatibus saepe eveniet ut et voluptates repudiandae sint et molestiae non recusandae. Itaque earum rerum hic tenetur a sapiente delectus, ut aut reiciendis voluptatibus maiores alias consequatur aut perferendis doloribus asperiores repellat."

1914 translation by H. Rackham

"On the other hand, we denounce with righteous indignation and dislike men who are so beguiled and demoralized by the charms of pleasure of the moment, so blinded by desire, that they cannot foresee the pain and trouble that are bound to ensue; and equal blame belongs to those who fail in their duty through weakness of will, which is the same as saying through shrinking from toil and pain. These cases are perfectly simple and easy to distinguish. In a free hour, when our power of choice is untrammelled and when nothing prevents our being able to do what we like best, every pleasure is to be welcomed and every pain avoided. But in certain circumstances and owing to the claims of duty or the obligations of business it will frequently occur that pleasures have to be repudiated and annoyances accepted. The wise man therefore always holds in these matters to this principle of selection: he rejects pleasures to secure other greater pleasures, or else he endures pains to avoid worse pains."

What is Lorem Ipsum?

Lorem Ipsum is simply dummy text of the printing and typesetting industry. Lorem Ipsum has been the industry's standard dummy text ever since the 1500s, when an unknown printer took a galley of type and scrambled it to make a type specimen book. It has survived not only five centuries, but also the leap into electronic typesetting, remaining essentially unchanged. It was popularised in the 1960s with the release of Letraset sheets containing Lorem Ipsum passages, and more recently with desktop publishing software like Aldus PageMaker including versions of Lorem Ipsum.

Why do we use it?

It is a long established fact that a reader will be distracted by the readable content of a page when looking at its layout. The point of using Lorem Ipsum is that it has a more-or-less normal distribution of letters, as opposed to using 'Content here, content here', making it look like readable English. Many desktop publishing packages and web page editors now use Lorem Ipsum as their default model text, and a search for 'lorem ipsum' will uncover many web sites still in their infancy. Various versions have evolved over the years, sometimes by accident, sometimes on purpose (injected humour and the like).

Where does it come from?

Contrary to popular belief, Lorem Ipsum is not simply random text. It has roots in a piece of classical Latin literature from 45 BC, making it over 2000 years old. Richard McClintock, a Latin professor at Hampden-Sydney College in Virginia, looked up one of the more obscure Latin words, consectetur, from a Lorem Ipsum passage, and going through the cites of the word in classical literature, discovered the undoubtable source. Lorem Ipsum comes from sections 1.10.32 and 1.10.33 of "de Finibus Bonorum et Malorum" (The Extremes of Good and Evil) by Cicero, written in 45 BC. This book is a treatise on the theory of ethics, very popular during the Renaissance. The first line of Lorem Ipsum, "Lorem ipsum dolor sit amet..", comes from a line in section 1.10.32.

The standard chunk of Lorem Ipsum used since the 1500s is reproduced below for those interested. Sections 1.10.32 and 1.10.33 from "de Finibus Bonorum et Malorum" by Cicero are also reproduced in their exact original form, accompanied by English versions from the 1914 translation by H. Rackham.

Where can I get some?

There are many variations of passages of Lorem Ipsum available, but the majority have suffered alteration in some form, by injected humour, or randomised words which don't look even slightly believable. If you are going to use a passage of Lorem Ipsum, you need to be sure there isn't anything embarrassing hidden in the middle of text. All the Lorem Ipsum generators on the Internet tend to repeat predefined chunks as necessary, making this the first true generator on the Internet. It uses a dictionary of over 200 Latin words, combined with a handful of model sentence

structures, to generate Lorem Ipsum which looks reasonable. The generated Lorem Ipsum is therefore always free from repetition, injected humour, or non-characteristic words etc.

The standard Lorem Ipsum passage, used since the 1500s

"Lorem ipsum dolor sit amet, consectetur adipiscing elit, sed do eiusmod tempor incididunt ut labore et dolore magna aliqua. Ut enim ad minim veniam, quis nostrud exercitation ullamco laboris nisi ut aliquip ex ea commodo consequat. Duis aute irure dolor in reprehenderit in voluptate velit esse cillum dolore eu fugiat nulla pariatur. Excepteur sint occaecat cupidatat non proident, sunt in culpa qui officia deserunt mollit anim id est laborum."

Section 1.10.32 of "de Finibus Bonorum et Malorum", written by Cicero in 45 BC

"Sed ut perspiciatis unde omnis iste natus error sit voluptatem accusantium doloremque laudantium, totam rem aperiam, eaque ipsa quae ab illo inventore veritatis et quasi architecto beatae vitae dicta sunt explicabo. Nemo enim ipsam voluptatem quia voluptas sit aspernatur aut odit aut fugit, sed quia consequuntur magni dolores eos qui ratione voluptatem sequi nesciunt. Neque porro quisquam est, qui dolorem ipsum quia dolor sit amet, consectetur, adipisci velit, sed quia non numquam eius modi tempora incidunt ut labore et dolore magnam aliquam quaerat voluptatem. Ut enim ad minima veniam, quis nostrum exercitationem ullam corporis suscipit laboriosam, nisi ut aliquid ex ea commodi consequatur? Quis autem vel eum iure reprehenderit qui in ea voluptate velit esse quam nihil molestiae consequatur, vel illum qui dolorem eum fugiat quo voluptas nulla pariatur?"

1914 translation by H. Rackham

"But I must explain to you how all this mistaken idea of denouncing pleasure and praising pain was born and I will give you a complete account of the system, and expound the actual teachings of the great explorer of the truth, the master-builder of human happiness. No one rejects, dislikes, or avoids pleasure itself, because it is pleasure, but because those who do not know how to pursue pleasure rationally encounter consequences that are extremely painful. Nor again is there anyone who loves or pursues or desires to obtain pain of itself, because it is pain, but because occasionally circumstances occur in which toil and pain can procure him some great pleasure. To take a trivial example, which of us ever undertakes laborious physical exercise, except to obtain some advantage from it? But who has any right to find fault with a man who chooses to enjoy a pleasure that has no annoying consequences, or one who avoids a pain that produces no resultant pleasure?"

Section 1.10.33 of "de Finibus Bonorum et Malorum", written by Cicero in 45 BC

"At vero eos et accusamus et iusto odio dignissimos ducimus qui blanditiis praesentium voluptatum deleniti atque corrupti quos dolores et quas molestias excepturi sint occaecati cupiditate non provident, similique sunt in culpa qui officia deserunt mollitia animi, id est laborum et dolorum fuga. Et harum quidem rerum facilis est et expedita distinctio. Nam libero tempore, cum soluta nobis est eligendi optio cumque nihil impedit quo minus id quod maxime placeat facere possimus, omnis voluptas assumenda est, omnis dolor repellendus. Temporibus autem quibusdam et aut officiis debitis aut rerum necessitatibus saepe eveniet ut et voluptates repudiandae sint et molestiae non recusandae. Itaque earum rerum hic

tenetur a sapiente delectus, ut aut reiciendis voluptatibus maiores alias consequatur aut perferendis doloribus asperiores repellat."

1914 translation by H. Rackham

"On the other hand, we denounce with righteous indignation and dislike men who are so beguiled and demoralized by the charms of pleasure of the moment, so blinded by desire, that they cannot foresee the pain and trouble that are bound to ensue; and equal blame belongs to those who fail in their duty through weakness of will, which is the same as saying through shrinking from toil and pain. These cases are perfectly simple and easy to distinguish. In a free hour, when our power of choice is untrammelled and when nothing prevents our being able to do what we like best, every pleasure is to be welcomed and every pain avoided. But in certain circumstances and owing to the claims of duty or the obligations of business it will frequently occur that pleasures have to be repudiated and annoyances accepted. The wise man therefore always holds in these matters to this principle of selection: he rejects pleasures to secure other greater pleasures, or else he endures pains to avoid worse pains."

What is Lorem Ipsum?

Lorem Ipsum is simply dummy text of the printing and typesetting industry. Lorem Ipsum has been the industry's standard dummy text ever since the 1500s, when an unknown printer took a galley of type and scrambled it to make a type specimen book. It has survived not only five centuries, but also the leap into electronic typesetting, remaining essentially unchanged. It was popularised in the 1960s with the release of Letraset sheets containing Lorem Ipsum passages, and more recently with desktop publishing software like Aldus PageMaker including versions of Lorem

Ipsum.

Why do we use it?

It is a long established fact that a reader will be distracted by the readable content of a page when looking at its layout. The point of using Lorem Ipsum is that it has a more-or-less normal distribution of letters, as opposed to using 'Content here, content here', making it look like readable English. Many desktop publishing packages and web page editors now use Lorem Ipsum as their default model text, and a search for 'lorem ipsum' will uncover many web sites still in their infancy. Various versions have evolved over the years, sometimes by accident, sometimes on purpose (injected humour and the like).

Where does it come from?

Contrary to popular belief, Lorem Ipsum is not simply random text. It has roots in a piece of classical Latin literature from 45 BC, making it over 2000 years old. Richard McClintock, a Latin professor at Hampden-Sydney College in Virginia, looked up one of the more obscure Latin words, consectetur, from a Lorem Ipsum passage, and going through the cites of the word in classical literature, discovered the undoubtable source. Lorem Ipsum comes from sections 1.10.32 and 1.10.33 of "de Finibus Bonorum et Malorum" (The Extremes of Good and Evil) by Cicero, written in 45 BC. This book is a treatise on the theory of ethics, very popular during the Renaissance. The first line of Lorem Ipsum, "Lorem ipsum dolor sit amet..", comes from a line in section 1.10.32.

The standard chunk of Lorem Ipsum used since the 1500s is reproduced below for those interested. Sections 1.10.32 and 1.10.33 from "de Finibus Bonorum et Malorum" by Cicero are also reproduced in their exact

original form, accompanied by English versions from the 1914 translation by H. Rackham.

Where can I get some?

There are many variations of passages of Lorem Ipsum available, but the majority have suffered alteration in some form, by injected humour, or randomised words which don't look even slightly believable. If you are going to use a passage of Lorem Ipsum, you need to be sure there isn't anything embarrassing hidden in the middle of text. All the Lorem Ipsum generators on the Internet tend to repeat predefined chunks as necessary, making this the first true generator on the Internet. It uses a dictionary of over 200 Latin words, combined with a handful of model sentence structures, to generate Lorem Ipsum which looks reasonable. The generated Lorem Ipsum is therefore always free from repetition, injected humour, or non-characteristic words etc.

The standard Lorem Ipsum passage, used since the 1500s

"Lorem ipsum dolor sit amet, consectetur adipiscing elit, sed do eiusmod tempor incididunt ut labore et dolore magna aliqua. Ut enim ad minim veniam, quis nostrud exercitation ullamco laboris nisi ut aliquip ex ea commodo consequat. Duis aute irure dolor in reprehenderit in voluptate velit esse cillum dolore eu fugiat nulla pariatur. Excepteur sint occaecat cupidatat non proident, sunt in culpa qui officia deserunt mollit anim id est laborum."

Section 1.10.32 of "de Finibus Bonorum et Malorum", written by Cicero in 45 BC

"Sed ut perspiciatis unde omnis iste natus error sit voluptatem accusantium doloremque laudantium, totam rem aperiam, eaque ipsa quae ab illo inventore veritatis et quasi architecto beatae vitae dicta sunt explicabo. Nemo

enim ipsam voluptatem quia voluptas sit aspernatur aut odit aut fugit, sed quia consequuntur magni dolores eos qui ratione voluptatem sequi nesciunt. Neque porro quisquam est, qui dolorem ipsum quia dolor sit amet, consectetur, adipisci velit, sed quia non numquam eius modi tempora incidunt ut labore et dolore magnam aliquam quaerat voluptatem. Ut enim ad minima veniam, quis nostrum exercitationem ullam corporis suscipit laboriosam, nisi ut aliquid ex ea commodi consequatur? Quis autem vel eum iure reprehenderit qui in ea voluptate velit esse quam nihil molestiae consequatur, vel illum qui dolorem eum fugiat quo voluptas nulla pariatur?"

1914 translation by H. Rackham

"But I must explain to you how all this mistaken idea of denouncing pleasure and praising pain was born and I will give you a complete account of the system, and expound the actual teachings of the great explorer of the truth, the master-builder of human happiness. No one rejects, dislikes, or avoids pleasure itself, because it is pleasure, but because those who do not know how to pursue pleasure rationally encounter consequences that are extremely painful. Nor again is there anyone who loves or pursues or desires to obtain pain of itself, because it is pain, but because occasionally circumstances occur in which toil and pain can procure him some great pleasure. To take a trivial example, which of us ever undertakes laborious physical exercise, except to obtain some advantage from it? But who has any right to find fault with a man who chooses to enjoy a pleasure that has no annoying consequences, or one who avoids a pain that produces no resultant pleasure?"

Section 1.10.33 of "de Finibus Bonorum et Malorum", written by Cicero in 45 BC

"At vero eos et accusamus et iusto odio dignissimos

ducimus qui blanditiis praesentium voluptatum deleniti atque corrupti quos dolores et quas molestias excepturi sint occaecati cupiditate non provident, similique sunt in culpa qui officia deserunt mollitia animi, id est laborum et dolorum fuga. Et harum quidem rerum facilis est et expedita distinctio. Nam libero tempore, cum soluta nobis est eligendi optio cumque nihil impedit quo minus id quod maxime placeat facere possimus, omnis voluptas assumenda est, omnis dolor repellendus. Temporibus autem quibusdam et aut officiis debitis aut rerum necessitatibus saepe eveniet ut et voluptates repudiandae sint et molestiae non recusandae. Itaque earum rerum hic tenetur a sapiente delectus, ut aut reiciendis voluptatibus maiores alias consequatur aut perferendis doloribus asperiores repellat."

1914 translation by H. Rackham
"On the other hand, we denounce with righteous indignation and dislike men who are so beguiled and demoralized by the charms of pleasure of the moment, so blinded by desire, that they cannot foresee the pain and trouble that are bound to ensue; and equal blame belongs to those who fail in their duty through weakness of will, which is the same as saying through shrinking from toil and pain. These cases are perfectly simple and easy to distinguish. In a free hour, when our power of choice is untrammelled and when nothing prevents our being able to do what we like best, every pleasure is to be welcomed and every pain avoided. But in certain circumstances and owing to the claims of duty or the obligations of business it will frequently occur that pleasures have to be repudiated and annoyances accepted. The wise man therefore always holds in these matters to this principle of selection: he rejects pleasures to secure other greater pleasures, or else

he endures pains to avoid worse pains."

What is Lorem Ipsum?

Lorem Ipsum is simply dummy text of the printing and typesetting industry. Lorem Ipsum has been the industry's standard dummy text ever since the 1500s, when an unknown printer took a galley of type and scrambled it to make a type specimen book. It has survived not only five centuries, but also the leap into electronic typesetting, remaining essentially unchanged. It was popularised in the 1960s with the release of Letraset sheets containing Lorem Ipsum passages, and more recently with desktop publishing software like Aldus PageMaker including versions of Lorem Ipsum.

Why do we use it?

It is a long established fact that a reader will be distracted by the readable content of a page when looking at its layout. The point of using Lorem Ipsum is that it has a more-or-less normal distribution of letters, as opposed to using 'Content here, content here', making it look like readable English. Many desktop publishing packages and web page editors now use Lorem Ipsum as their default model text, and a search for 'lorem ipsum' will uncover many web sites still in their infancy. Various versions have evolved over the years, sometimes by accident, sometimes on purpose (injected humour and the like).

Where does it come from?

Contrary to popular belief, Lorem Ipsum is not simply random text. It has roots in a piece of classical Latin literature from 45 BC, making it over 2000 years old. Richard McClintock, a Latin professor at Hampden-Sydney College in Virginia, looked up one of the more obscure Latin words, consectetur, from a Lorem Ipsum passage, and going through the cites of the word in classical literature, discovered the undoubtable source. Lorem Ipsum comes from sections 1.10.32 and 1.10.33 of "de Finibus Bonorum et Malorum" (The Extremes of Good and Evil) by Cicero, written in 45 BC. This book is a treatise on the theory of ethics, very popular during the Renaissance. The first line of Lorem Ipsum, "Lorem ipsum dolor sit amet..", comes from a line in section 1.10.32.

The standard chunk of Lorem Ipsum used since the 1500s is reproduced below for those interested. Sections 1.10.32 and 1.10.33 from "de Finibus Bonorum et Malorum" by Cicero are also reproduced in their exact original form, accompanied by English versions from the 1914 translation by H. Rackham.

Where can I get some?

There are many variations of passages of Lorem Ipsum available, but the majority have suffered alteration in some form, by injected humour, or randomised words which don't look even slightly believable. If you are going to use a passage of Lorem Ipsum, you need to be sure there isn't anything embarrassing hidden in the middle of text. All the Lorem Ipsum generators on the Internet tend to repeat predefined chunks as necessary, making this the first true generator on the Internet. It uses a dictionary of over 200 Latin words, combined with a handful of model sentence structures, to generate Lorem Ipsum which looks reasonable. The generated Lorem Ipsum is therefore always free from repetition, injected humour, or non-characteristic words etc.

The standard Lorem Ipsum passage, used since the 1500s

"Lorem ipsum dolor sit amet, consectetur adipiscing elit, sed do eiusmod tempor incididunt ut labore et dolore magna aliqua. Ut enim ad minim veniam, quis nostrud exercitation ullamco laboris nisi ut aliquip ex ea commodo consequat. Duis aute irure dolor in reprehenderit in voluptate velit esse cillum dolore eu fugiat nulla pariatur. Excepteur sint occaecat cupidatat non proident, sunt in culpa qui officia deserunt mollit anim id est laborum."

Section 1.10.32 of "de Finibus Bonorum et Malorum", written by Cicero in 45 BC

"Sed ut perspiciatis unde omnis iste natus error sit voluptatem accusantium doloremque laudantium, totam rem aperiam, eaque ipsa quae ab illo inventore veritatis et quasi architecto beatae vitae dicta sunt explicabo. Nemo enim ipsam voluptatem quia voluptas sit aspernatur aut odit aut fugit, sed quia consequuntur magni dolores eos qui ratione voluptatem sequi nesciunt. Neque porro quisquam est, qui dolorem ipsum quia dolor sit amet, consectetur, adipisci velit, sed quia non numquam eius modi tempora incidunt ut labore et dolore magnam aliquam quaerat voluptatem. Ut enim ad minima veniam, quis nostrum exercitationem ullam corporis suscipit laboriosam, nisi ut aliquid ex ea commodi consequatur? Quis autem vel eum iure reprehenderit qui in ea voluptate velit esse quam nihil molestiae consequatur, vel illum qui dolorem eum fugiat quo voluptas nulla pariatur?"

1914 translation by H. Rackham

"But I must explain to you how all this mistaken idea of denouncing pleasure and praising pain was born and I will give you a complete account of the system, and expound the actual teachings of the great explorer of the truth, the master-builder of human happiness. No one rejects, dislikes, or avoids pleasure itself, because it is pleasure, but because those who do not know how to pursue pleasure rationally encounter consequences that are extremely painful. Nor again is there anyone who loves or pursues or desires to obtain pain of itself, because it is pain, but because occasionally circumstances occur in which toil and pain can procure him some great pleasure. To take a trivial example, which of us ever undertakes laborious physical exercise, except to obtain some advantage from it? But who has any right to find fault with a man who chooses to enjoy a pleasure that has no annoying consequences, or one who avoids a pain that produces no resultant pleasure?"

Section 1.10.33 of "de Finibus Bonorum et Malorum", written by Cicero in 45 BC

"At vero eos et accusamus et iusto odio dignissimos ducimus qui blanditiis praesentium voluptatum deleniti atque corrupti quos dolores et quas molestias excepturi sint occaecati cupiditate non provident, similique sunt in culpa qui officia deserunt mollitia animi, id est laborum et dolorum fuga. Et harum quidem rerum facilis est et expedita distinctio. Nam libero tempore, cum soluta nobis est eligendi optio cumque nihil impedit quo minus id quod maxime placeat facere possimus, omnis voluptas assumenda est, omnis dolor repellendus. Temporibus autem quibusdam et aut officiis debitis aut rerum necessitatibus saepe eveniet ut et voluptates repudiandae sint et molestiae non recusandae. Itaque earum rerum hic tenetur a sapiente delectus, ut aut reiciendis voluptatibus maiores alias consequatur aut perferendis doloribus asperiores repellat."

1914 translation by H. Rackham

"On the other hand, we denounce with righteous indignation and dislike men who are so beguiled and demoralized by the charms of pleasure of the moment, so blinded by desire, that they cannot foresee the pain and trouble that are bound to ensue; and equal blame belongs to those who fail in their duty through weakness of will, which is the same as saying through shrinking from toil and pain. These cases are perfectly simple and easy to distinguish. In a free hour, when our power of choice is untrammelled and when nothing prevents our being able to do what we like best, every pleasure is to be welcomed and every pain avoided. But in certain circumstances and owing to the claims of duty or the obligations of business it will frequently occur that pleasures have to be repudiated and annoyances accepted. The wise man therefore always holds in these matters to this principle of selection: he rejects pleasures to secure other greater pleasures, or else he endures pains to avoid worse pains."

What is Lorem Ipsum?

Lorem Ipsum is simply dummy text of the printing and typesetting industry. Lorem Ipsum has been the industry's standard dummy text ever since the 1500s, when an unknown printer took a galley of type and scrambled it to make a type specimen book. It has survived not only five centuries, but also the leap into electronic typesetting, remaining essentially unchanged. It was popularised in the 1960s with the release of Letraset sheets containing Lorem Ipsum passages, and more recently with desktop publishing software like Aldus PageMaker including versions of Lorem Ipsum.

Why do we use it?

It is a long established fact that a reader will be distracted by the readable content of a page when looking at its layout. The point of using Lorem Ipsum is that it has a more-or-less normal distribution of letters, as opposed to using 'Content here, content here', making it look like readable English. Many desktop publishing packages and web page editors now use Lorem Ipsum as their default model text, and a search for 'lorem ipsum' will uncover many web sites still in their infancy. Various versions have evolved over the years, sometimes by accident, sometimes on purpose (injected humour and the like).

Where does it come from?
Contrary to popular belief, Lorem Ipsum is not simply random text. It has roots in a piece of classical Latin literature from 45 BC, making it over 2000 years old. Richard McClintock, a Latin professor at Hampden-Sydney College in Virginia, looked up one of the more obscure Latin words, consectetur, from a Lorem Ipsum passage, and going through the cites of the word in classical literature, discovered the undoubtable source. Lorem Ipsum comes from sections 1.10.32 and 1.10.33 of "de Finibus Bonorum et Malorum" (The Extremes of Good and Evil) by Cicero, written in 45 BC. This book is a treatise on the theory of ethics, very popular during the Renaissance. The first line of Lorem Ipsum, "Lorem ipsum dolor sit amet..", comes from a line in section 1.10.32.

The standard chunk of Lorem Ipsum used since the 1500s is reproduced below for those interested. Sections 1.10.32 and 1.10.33 from "de Finibus Bonorum et Malorum" by Cicero are also reproduced in their exact original form, accompanied by English versions from the 1914 translation by H. Rackham.

Where can I get some?
There are many variations of passages of Lorem Ipsum available, but the majority have suffered alteration in some form, by injected humour, or randomised words which don't look even slightly believable. If you are going to use a passage of Lorem Ipsum, you need to be sure there isn't anything embarrassing hidden in the middle of text. All

the Lorem Ipsum generators on the Internet tend to repeat predefined chunks as necessary, making this the first true generator on the Internet. It uses a dictionary of over 200 Latin words, combined with a handful of model sentence structures, to generate Lorem Ipsum which looks reasonable. The generated Lorem Ipsum is therefore always free from repetition, injected humour, or non-characteristic words etc.

The standard Lorem Ipsum passage, used since the 1500s

"Lorem ipsum dolor sit amet, consectetur adipiscing elit, sed do eiusmod tempor incididunt ut labore et dolore magna aliqua. Ut enim ad minim veniam, quis nostrud exercitation ullamco laboris nisi ut aliquip ex ea commodo consequat. Duis aute irure dolor in reprehenderit in voluptate velit esse cillum dolore eu fugiat nulla pariatur. Excepteur sint occaecat cupidatat non proident, sunt in culpa qui officia deserunt mollit anim id est laborum."

Section 1.10.32 of "de Finibus Bonorum et Malorum", written by Cicero in 45 BC

"Sed ut perspiciatis unde omnis iste natus error sit voluptatem accusantium doloremque laudantium, totam rem aperiam, eaque ipsa quae ab illo inventore veritatis et quasi architecto beatae vitae dicta sunt explicabo. Nemo enim ipsam voluptatem quia voluptas sit aspernatur aut odit aut fugit, sed quia consequuntur magni dolores eos qui ratione voluptatem sequi nesciunt. Neque porro quisquam est, qui dolorem ipsum quia dolor sit amet, consectetur, adipisci velit, sed quia non numquam eius modi tempora incidunt ut labore et dolore magnam aliquam quaerat voluptatem. Ut enim ad minima veniam, quis nostrum exercitationem ullam corporis suscipit laboriosam, nisi ut aliquid ex ea commodi consequatur? Quis autem vel eum iure reprehenderit qui in ea voluptate velit esse quam nihil molestiae consequatur, vel illum qui dolorem eum fugiat quo voluptas nulla pariatur?"

1914 translation by H. Rackham

"But I must explain to you how all this mistaken idea of denouncing pleasure and praising pain was born and I will give you a complete account of the system, and expound the actual teachings of the great explorer of the truth, the master-builder of human happiness. No one rejects, dislikes, or avoids pleasure itself, because it is pleasure, but because those who do not know how to pursue pleasure rationally encounter consequences that are extremely painful. Nor again is there anyone who loves or pursues or desires to obtain pain of itself, because it is pain, but because occasionally circumstances occur in which toil and pain can procure him some great pleasure. To take a trivial example, which of us ever undertakes laborious physical exercise, except to obtain some advantage from it? But who has any right to find fault with a man who chooses to enjoy a pleasure that has no annoying consequences, or one who avoids a pain that produces no resultant pleasure?"

Section 1.10.33 of "de Finibus Bonorum et Malorum", written by Cicero in 45 BC

"At vero eos et accusamus et iusto odio dignissimos ducimus qui blanditiis praesentium voluptatum deleniti atque corrupti quos dolores et quas molestias excepturi sint occaecati cupiditate non provident, similique sunt in culpa qui officia deserunt mollitia animi, id est laborum et dolorum fuga. Et harum quidem rerum facilis est et expedita distinctio. Nam libero tempore, cum soluta nobis est eligendi optio cumque nihil impedit quo minus id quod maxime placeat facere possimus, omnis voluptas assumenda est, omnis dolor repellendus. Temporibus autem quibusdam et aut officiis debitis aut rerum necessitatibus saepe eveniet ut et voluptates repudiandae sint et molestiae non recusandae. Itaque earum rerum hic tenetur a sapiente delectus, ut aut reiciendis voluptatibus maiores alias consequatur aut perferendis doloribus asperiores repellat."

1914 translation by H. Rackham

"On the other hand, we denounce with righteous indignation and dislike men who are so beguiled and demoralized by the charms of pleasure of the moment, so blinded by desire, that they cannot foresee the pain and trouble that are bound to ensue; and equal blame belongs to those who fail in their duty through weakness of will, which is the same as saying through shrinking from toil and pain. These cases are perfectly simple and easy to distinguish. In a free hour, when our power of choice is untrammelled and when nothing prevents our being able to do what we like best, every pleasure is to be welcomed and every pain avoided. But in certain circumstances and owing to the claims of duty or the obligations of business it will frequently occur that pleasures have to be repudiated and annoyances accepted. The wise man therefore always holds in these matters to this principle of selection: he rejects pleasures to secure other greater pleasures, or else he endures pains to avoid worse pains."

What is Lorem Ipsum?

Lorem Ipsum is simply dummy text of the printing and typesetting industry. Lorem Ipsum has been the industry's standard dummy text ever since the 1500s, when an unknown printer took a galley of type and scrambled it to make a type specimen book. It has survived not only five centuries, but also the leap into electronic typesetting, remaining essentially unchanged. It was popularised in the

1960s with the release of Letraset sheets containing Lorem Ipsum passages, and more recently with desktop publishing software like Aldus PageMaker including versions of Lorem Ipsum.

Why do we use it?

It is a long established fact that a reader will be distracted by the readable content of a page when looking at its layout. The point of using Lorem Ipsum is that it has a more-or-less normal distribution of letters, as opposed to using 'Content here, content here', making it look like readable English. Many desktop publishing packages and web page editors now use Lorem Ipsum as their default model text, and a search for 'lorem ipsum' will uncover many web sites still in their infancy. Various versions have evolved over the years, sometimes by accident, sometimes on purpose (injected humour and the like).

Where does it come from?

Contrary to popular belief, Lorem Ipsum is not simply random text. It has roots in a piece of classical Latin literature from 45 BC, making it over 2000 years old. Richard McClintock, a Latin professor at Hampden-Sydney College in Virginia, looked up one of the more obscure Latin words, consectetur, from a Lorem Ipsum passage, and going through the cites of the word in classical literature, discovered the undoubtable source. Lorem Ipsum comes from sections 1.10.32 and 1.10.33 of "de Finibus Bonorum et Malorum" (The Extremes of Good and Evil) by Cicero, written in 45 BC. This book is a treatise on the theory of ethics, very popular during the Renaissance. The first line of Lorem Ipsum, "Lorem ipsum dolor sit amet..", comes from a line in section 1.10.32.

The standard chunk of Lorem Ipsum used since the 1500s is reproduced below for those interested. Sections 1.10.32 and 1.10.33 from "de Finibus Bonorum et Malorum" by Cicero are also reproduced in their exact original form, accompanied by English versions from the 1914 translation by H. Rackham.

Where can I get some?
There are many variations of passages of Lorem Ipsum available, but the majority have suffered alteration in some form, by injected humour, or randomised words which don't look even slightly believable. If you are going to use a passage of Lorem Ipsum, you need to be sure there isn't anything embarrassing hidden in the middle of text. All the Lorem Ipsum generators on the Internet tend to repeat predefined chunks as necessary, making this the first true generator on the Internet. It uses a dictionary of over 200 Latin words, combined with a handful of model sentence structures, to generate Lorem Ipsum which looks reasonable. The generated Lorem Ipsum is therefore always free from repetition, injected humour, or non-characteristic words etc.

The standard Lorem Ipsum passage, used since the 1500s
"Lorem ipsum dolor sit amet, consectetur adipiscing elit, sed do eiusmod tempor incididunt ut labore et dolore magna aliqua. Ut enim ad minim veniam, quis nostrud exercitation ullamco laboris nisi ut aliquip ex ea commodo consequat. Duis aute irure dolor in reprehenderit in voluptate velit esse cillum dolore eu fugiat nulla pariatur. Excepteur sint occaecat cupidatat non proident, sunt in culpa qui officia deserunt mollit anim id est laborum."

Section 1.10.32 of "de Finibus Bonorum et Malorum", written by Cicero in 45 BC

"Sed ut perspiciatis unde omnis iste natus error sit voluptatem accusantium doloremque laudantium, totam rem aperiam, eaque ipsa quae ab illo inventore veritatis et quasi architecto beatae vitae dicta sunt explicabo. Nemo enim ipsam voluptatem quia voluptas sit aspernatur aut odit aut fugit, sed quia consequuntur magni dolores eos qui ratione voluptatem sequi nesciunt. Neque porro quisquam est, qui dolorem ipsum quia dolor sit amet, consectetur, adipisci velit, sed quia non numquam eius modi tempora incidunt ut labore et dolore magnam aliquam quaerat voluptatem. Ut enim ad minima veniam, quis nostrum exercitationem ullam corporis suscipit laboriosam, nisi ut aliquid ex ea commodi consequatur? Quis autem vel eum iure reprehenderit qui in ea voluptate velit esse quam nihil molestiae consequatur, vel illum qui dolorem eum fugiat quo voluptas nulla pariatur?"

1914 translation by H. Rackham

"But I must explain to you how all this mistaken idea of denouncing pleasure and praising pain was born and I will give you a complete account of the system, and expound the actual teachings of the great explorer of the truth, the master-builder of human happiness. No one rejects, dislikes, or avoids pleasure itself, because it is pleasure, but because those who do not know how to pursue pleasure rationally encounter consequences that are extremely painful. Nor again is there anyone who loves or pursues or desires to obtain pain of itself, because it is pain, but because occasionally circumstances occur in which toil and pain can procure him some great pleasure. To take a trivial example, which of us ever undertakes laborious physical exercise, except to obtain some advantage from it? But who has any right to find fault with a man who chooses to enjoy a pleasure that has no annoying consequences, or one who avoids a pain that produces no resultant pleasure?"

Section 1.10.33 of "de Finibus Bonorum et Malorum", written by Cicero in 45 BC

"At vero eos et accusamus et iusto odio dignissimos ducimus qui blanditiis praesentium voluptatum deleniti atque corrupti quos dolores et quas molestias excepturi sint occaecati cupiditate non provident, similique sunt in culpa qui officia deserunt mollitia animi, id est laborum et dolorum fuga. Et harum quidem rerum facilis est et expedita distinctio. Nam libero tempore, cum soluta nobis est eligendi optio cumque nihil impedit quo minus id quod maxime placeat facere possimus, omnis voluptas assumenda est, omnis dolor repellendus. Temporibus autem quibusdam et aut officiis debitis aut rerum necessitatibus saepe eveniet ut et voluptates repudiandae sint et molestiae non recusandae. Itaque earum rerum hic tenetur a sapiente delectus, ut aut reiciendis voluptatibus maiores alias consequatur aut perferendis doloribus asperiores repellat."

1914 translation by H. Rackham

"On the other hand, we denounce with righteous indignation and dislike men who are so beguiled and demoralized by the charms of pleasure of the moment, so blinded by desire, that they cannot foresee the pain and trouble that are bound to ensue; and equal blame belongs to those who fail in their duty through weakness of will, which is the same as saying through shrinking from toil and pain. These cases are perfectly simple and easy to distinguish. In a free hour, when our power of choice is untrammelled and when nothing prevents our being able to do what we like best, every pleasure is to be welcomed and every pain avoided. But in certain circumstances and owing to the claims of duty or the obligations of business it will frequently occur that pleasures have to be repudiated and annoyances accepted. The wise man therefore always holds in these matters to this principle of selection: he rejects pleasures to secure other greater pleasures, or else he endures pains to avoid worse pains."

What is Lorem Ipsum?

Lorem Ipsum is simply dummy text of the printing and typesetting industry. Lorem Ipsum has been the industry's standard dummy text ever since the 1500s, when an unknown printer took a galley of type and scrambled it to make a type specimen book. It has survived not only five centuries, but also the leap into electronic typesetting, remaining essentially unchanged. It was popularised in the 1960s with the release of Letraset sheets containing Lorem Ipsum passages, and more recently with desktop publishing software like Aldus PageMaker including versions of Lorem Ipsum.

Why do we use it?

It is a long established fact that a reader will be distracted by the readable content of a page when looking at its layout. The point of using Lorem Ipsum is that it has a more-or-less normal distribution of letters, as opposed to using 'Content here, content here', making it look like readable English. Many desktop publishing packages and web page editors now use Lorem Ipsum as their default model text, and a search for 'lorem ipsum' will uncover many web sites still in their infancy. Various versions have evolved over the years, sometimes by accident, sometimes on purpose (injected humour and the like).

Where does it come from?

Contrary to popular belief, Lorem Ipsum is not simply random text. It has roots in a piece of classical Latin literature from 45 BC, making it over 2000 years old. Richard McClintock, a Latin professor at Hampden-Sydney College in Virginia, looked up one of the more obscure Latin words, consectetur, from a Lorem Ipsum passage, and going through the cites of the word in classical literature, discovered the undoubtable source. Lorem Ipsum comes from sections 1.10.32 and 1.10.33 of "de Finibus Bonorum et Malorum" (The Extremes of Good and Evil) by Cicero, written in 45 BC. This book is a treatise on the theory of ethics, very popular during the Renaissance. The first line of Lorem Ipsum, "Lorem ipsum dolor sit amet..", comes from a line in section 1.10.32.

The standard chunk of Lorem Ipsum used since the 1500s is reproduced below for those interested. Sections 1.10.32 and 1.10.33 from "de Finibus Bonorum et Malorum" by Cicero are also reproduced in their exact original form, accompanied by English versions from the 1914 translation by H. Rackham.

Where can I get some?

There are many variations of passages of Lorem Ipsum available, but the majority have suffered alteration in some form, by injected humour, or randomised words which don't look even slightly believable. If you are going to use a passage of Lorem Ipsum, you need to be sure there isn't anything embarrassing hidden in the middle of text. All the Lorem Ipsum generators on the Internet tend to repeat predefined chunks as necessary, making this the first true generator on the Internet. It uses a dictionary of over 200 Latin words, combined with a handful of model sentence structures, to generate Lorem Ipsum which looks reasonable. The generated Lorem Ipsum is therefore always free from repetition, injected humour, or non-characteristic words etc.

The standard Lorem Ipsum passage, used since the 1500s

"Lorem ipsum dolor sit amet, consectetur adipiscing elit, sed do eiusmod tempor incididunt ut labore et dolore magna aliqua. Ut enim ad minim veniam, quis nostrud exercitation ullamco laboris nisi ut aliquip ex ea commodo consequat. Duis aute irure dolor in reprehenderit in voluptate velit esse cillum dolore eu fugiat nulla pariatur. Excepteur sint occaecat cupidatat non proident, sunt in culpa qui officia deserunt mollit anim id est laborum."

Section 1.10.32 of "de Finibus Bonorum et Malorum", written by Cicero in 45 BC

"Sed ut perspiciatis unde omnis iste natus error sit voluptatem accusantium doloremque laudantium, totam rem aperiam, eaque ipsa quae ab illo inventore veritatis et quasi architecto beatae vitae dicta sunt explicabo. Nemo enim ipsam voluptatem quia voluptas sit aspernatur aut odit aut fugit, sed quia consequuntur magni dolores eos qui ratione voluptatem sequi nesciunt. Neque porro quisquam est, qui dolorem ipsum quia dolor sit amet, consectetur, adipisci velit, sed quia non numquam eius modi tempora incidunt ut labore et dolore magnam aliquam quaerat voluptatem. Ut enim ad minima veniam, quis nostrum exercitationem ullam corporis suscipit laboriosam, nisi ut aliquid ex ea commodi consequatur? Quis autem vel eum iure reprehenderit qui in ea voluptate velit esse quam nihil molestiae consequatur, vel illum qui dolorem eum fugiat quo voluptas nulla pariatur?"

1914 translation by H. Rackham

"But I must explain to you how all this mistaken idea of denouncing pleasure and praising pain was born and I will give you a complete account of the system, and expound the actual teachings of the great explorer of the truth, the master-builder of human happiness. No one rejects, dislikes, or avoids pleasure itself, because it is pleasure, but because those who do not know how to pursue pleasure rationally encounter consequences that are extremely painful. Nor again is there anyone who loves or pursues or desires to obtain pain of itself, because it is pain, but because occasionally circumstances occur in which toil and pain can procure him some great pleasure. To take a trivial example, which of us ever undertakes laborious physical exercise, except to obtain some advantage from it? But who has any right to find fault with a man who chooses to enjoy a pleasure that has no annoying consequences, or one who avoids a pain that produces no resultant pleasure?"

Section 1.10.33 of "de Finibus Bonorum et Malorum", written by Cicero in 45 BC

"At vero eos et accusamus et iusto odio dignissimos ducimus qui blanditiis praesentium voluptatum deleniti atque corrupti quos dolores et quas molestias excepturi sint occaecati cupiditate non provident, similique sunt in culpa qui officia deserunt mollitia animi, id est laborum et dolorum fuga. Et harum quidem rerum facilis est et expedita distinctio. Nam libero tempore, cum soluta nobis est eligendi optio cumque nihil impedit quo minus id quod maxime placeat facere possimus, omnis voluptas assumenda est, omnis dolor repellendus. Temporibus autem quibusdam et aut officiis debitis aut rerum necessitatibus saepe eveniet ut et voluptates repudiandae sint et molestiae non recusandae. Itaque earum rerum hic tenetur a sapiente delectus, ut aut reiciendis voluptatibus maiores alias consequatur aut perferendis doloribus asperiores repellat."

1914 translation by H. Rackham

"On the other hand, we denounce with righteous

indignation and dislike men who are so beguiled and demoralized by the charms of pleasure of the moment, so blinded by desire, that they cannot foresee the pain and trouble that are bound to ensue; and equal blame belongs to those who fail in their duty through weakness of will, which is the same as saying through shrinking from toil and pain. These cases are perfectly simple and easy to distinguish. In a free hour, when our power of choice is untrammelled and when nothing prevents our being able to do what we like best, every pleasure is to be welcomed and every pain avoided. But in certain circumstances and owing to the claims of duty or the obligations of business it will frequently occur that pleasures have to be repudiated and annoyances accepted. The wise man therefore always holds in these matters to this principle of selection: he rejects pleasures to secure other greater pleasures, or else he endures pains to avoid worse pains."

What is Lorem Ipsum?

Lorem Ipsum is simply dummy text of the printing and typesetting industry. Lorem Ipsum has been the industry's standard dummy text ever since the 1500s, when an unknown printer took a galley of type and scrambled it to make a type specimen book. It has survived not only five centuries, but also the leap into electronic typesetting, remaining essentially unchanged. It was popularised in the 1960s with the release of Letraset sheets containing Lorem Ipsum passages, and more recently with desktop publishing software like Aldus PageMaker including versions of Lorem Ipsum.

Why do we use it?

It is a long established fact that a reader will be distracted by the readable content of a page when looking at its layout. The point of using Lorem Ipsum is that it has a more-or-less normal distribution of letters, as opposed to using 'Content here, content here', making it look like readable English. Many desktop publishing packages and web page editors now use Lorem Ipsum as their default model text, and a search for 'lorem ipsum' will uncover many web sites still in their infancy. Various versions have evolved over the years, sometimes by accident, sometimes on purpose (injected humour and the like).

Where does it come from?
Contrary to popular belief, Lorem Ipsum is not simply random text. It has roots in a piece of classical Latin literature from 45 BC, making it over 2000 years old. Richard McClintock, a Latin professor at Hampden-Sydney College in Virginia, looked up one of the more obscure Latin words, consectetur, from a Lorem Ipsum passage, and going through the cites of the word in classical literature, discovered the undoubtable source. Lorem Ipsum comes from sections 1.10.32 and 1.10.33 of "de Finibus Bonorum et Malorum" (The Extremes of Good and Evil) by Cicero, written in 45 BC. This book is a treatise on the theory of ethics, very popular during the Renaissance. The first line of Lorem Ipsum, "Lorem ipsum dolor sit amet..", comes from a line in section 1.10.32.

The standard chunk of Lorem Ipsum used since the 1500s is reproduced below for those interested. Sections 1.10.32 and 1.10.33 from "de Finibus Bonorum et Malorum" by Cicero are also reproduced in their exact original form, accompanied by English versions from the 1914 translation by H. Rackham.

Where can I get some?
There are many variations of passages of Lorem Ipsum available, but the majority have suffered alteration in some

form, by injected humour, or randomised words which don't look even slightly believable. If you are going to use a passage of Lorem Ipsum, you need to be sure there isn't anything embarrassing hidden in the middle of text. All the Lorem Ipsum generators on the Internet tend to repeat predefined chunks as necessary, making this the first true generator on the Internet. It uses a dictionary of over 200 Latin words, combined with a handful of model sentence structures, to generate Lorem Ipsum which looks reasonable. The generated Lorem Ipsum is therefore always free from repetition, injected humour, or non-characteristic words etc.

The standard Lorem Ipsum passage, used since the 1500s

"Lorem ipsum dolor sit amet, consectetur adipiscing elit, sed do eiusmod tempor incididunt ut labore et dolore magna aliqua. Ut enim ad minim veniam, quis nostrud exercitation ullamco laboris nisi ut aliquip ex ea commodo consequat. Duis aute irure dolor in reprehenderit in voluptate velit esse cillum dolore eu fugiat nulla pariatur. Excepteur sint occaecat cupidatat non proident, sunt in culpa qui officia deserunt mollit anim id est laborum."

Section 1.10.32 of "de Finibus Bonorum et Malorum", written by Cicero in 45 BC

"Sed ut perspiciatis unde omnis iste natus error sit voluptatem accusantium doloremque laudantium, totam rem aperiam, eaque ipsa quae ab illo inventore veritatis et quasi architecto beatae vitae dicta sunt explicabo. Nemo enim ipsam voluptatem quia voluptas sit aspernatur aut odit aut fugit, sed quia consequuntur magni dolores eos qui ratione voluptatem sequi nesciunt. Neque porro quisquam est, qui dolorem ipsum quia dolor sit amet, consectetur, adipisci velit, sed quia non numquam eius modi tempora incidunt ut labore et dolore magnam aliquam quaerat voluptatem. Ut enim ad minima veniam, quis nostrum exercitationem ullam corporis suscipit laboriosam, nisi ut aliquid ex ea commodi consequatur? Quis autem vel eum iure reprehenderit qui in ea voluptate velit esse quam nihil molestiae consequatur, vel illum qui dolorem eum fugiat quo voluptas nulla pariatur?"

1914 translation by H. Rackham

"But I must explain to you how all this mistaken idea of denouncing pleasure and praising pain was born and I will give you a complete account of the system, and expound the actual teachings of the great explorer of the truth, the master-builder of human happiness. No one rejects, dislikes, or avoids pleasure itself, because it is pleasure, but because those who do not know how to pursue pleasure rationally encounter consequences that are extremely painful. Nor again is there anyone who loves or pursues or desires to obtain pain of itself, because it is pain, but because occasionally circumstances occur in which toil and pain can procure him some great pleasure. To take a trivial example, which of us ever undertakes laborious physical exercise, except to obtain some advantage from it? But who has any right to find fault with a man who chooses to enjoy a pleasure that has no annoying consequences, or one who avoids a pain that produces no resultant pleasure?"

Section 1.10.33 of "de Finibus Bonorum et Malorum", written by Cicero in 45 BC

"At vero eos et accusamus et iusto odio dignissimos ducimus qui blanditiis praesentium voluptatum deleniti atque corrupti quos dolores et quas molestias excepturi sint occaecati cupiditate non provident, similique sunt in culpa qui officia deserunt mollitia animi, id est laborum et dolorum fuga. Et harum quidem rerum facilis est et expedita distinctio. Nam libero tempore, cum soluta nobis est eligendi optio cumque nihil impedit quo minus id quod maxime placeat facere possimus, omnis voluptas assumenda est, omnis dolor repellendus. Temporibus autem quibusdam et aut officiis debitis aut rerum necessitatibus saepe eveniet ut et voluptates repudiandae sint et molestiae non recusandae. Itaque earum rerum hic tenetur a sapiente delectus, ut aut reiciendis voluptatibus maiores alias consequatur aut perferendis doloribus asperiores repellat."

1914 translation by H. Rackham

"On the other hand, we denounce with righteous indignation and dislike men who are so beguiled and demoralized by the charms of pleasure of the moment, so blinded by desire, that they cannot foresee the pain and trouble that are bound to ensue; and equal blame belongs to those who fail in their duty through weakness of will, which is the same as saying through shrinking from toil and pain. These cases are perfectly simple and easy to distinguish. In a free hour, when our power of choice is untrammelled and when nothing prevents our being able to do what we like best, every pleasure is to be welcomed and every pain avoided. But in certain circumstances and owing to the claims of duty or the obligations of business it will frequently occur that pleasures have to be repudiated and annoyances accepted. The wise man therefore always holds in these matters to this principle of selection: he rejects pleasures to secure other greater pleasures, or else he endures pains to avoid worse pains."

What is Lorem Ipsum?

Lorem Ipsum is simply dummy text of the printing and typesetting industry. Lorem Ipsum has been the industry's standard dummy text ever since the 1500s, when an unknown printer took a galley of type and scrambled it to make a type specimen book. It has survived not only five centuries, but also the leap into electronic typesetting, remaining essentially unchanged. It was popularised in the 1960s with the release of Letraset sheets containing Lorem Ipsum passages, and more recently with desktop publishing software like Aldus PageMaker including versions of Lorem Ipsum.

Why do we use it?

It is a long established fact that a reader will be distracted by the readable content of a page when looking at its layout. The point of using Lorem Ipsum is that it has a more-or-less normal distribution of letters, as opposed to using 'Content here, content here', making it look like readable English. Many desktop publishing packages and web page editors now use Lorem Ipsum as their default model text, and a search for 'lorem ipsum' will uncover many web sites still in their infancy. Various versions have evolved over the years, sometimes by accident, sometimes on purpose (injected humour and the like).

Where does it come from?

Contrary to popular belief, Lorem Ipsum is not simply random text. It has roots in a piece of classical Latin literature from 45 BC, making it over 2000 years old. Richard McClintock, a Latin professor at Hampden-Sydney College in Virginia, looked up one of the more obscure Latin words, consectetur, from a Lorem Ipsum passage, and going through the cites of the word in classical literature, discovered the undoubtable source. Lorem Ipsum comes from sections 1.10.32 and 1.10.33 of "de Finibus Bonorum et Malorum" (The Extremes of Good and Evil) by Cicero, written in 45 BC. This book is a treatise on the theory of ethics, very popular during the Renaissance. The first line of Lorem Ipsum, "Lorem ipsum dolor sit amet..", comes from a line in section 1.10.32.

The standard chunk of Lorem Ipsum used since the 1500s is reproduced below for those interested. Sections 1.10.32 and 1.10.33 from "de Finibus Bonorum et Malorum" by Cicero are also reproduced in their exact original form, accompanied by English versions from the 1914 translation by H. Rackham.

Where can I get some?
There are many variations of passages of Lorem Ipsum available, but the majority have suffered alteration in some form, by injected humour, or randomised words which don't look even slightly believable. If you are going to use a passage of Lorem Ipsum, you need to be sure there isn't anything embarrassing hidden in the middle of text. All the Lorem Ipsum generators on the Internet tend to repeat predefined chunks as necessary, making this the first true generator on the Internet. It uses a dictionary of over 200 Latin words, combined with a handful of model sentence structures, to generate Lorem Ipsum which looks reasonable. The generated Lorem Ipsum is therefore always free from repetition, injected humour, or non-characteristic words etc.

The standard Lorem Ipsum passage, used since the 1500s
"Lorem ipsum dolor sit amet, consectetur adipiscing elit, sed do eiusmod tempor incididunt ut labore et dolore magna aliqua. Ut enim ad minim veniam, quis nostrud exercitation ullamco laboris nisi ut aliquip ex ea commodo consequat. Duis aute irure dolor in reprehenderit in voluptate velit esse cillum dolore eu fugiat nulla pariatur. Excepteur sint occaecat cupidatat non proident, sunt in

culpa qui officia deserunt mollit anim id est laborum."

Section 1.10.32 of "de Finibus Bonorum et Malorum", written by Cicero in 45 BC

"Sed ut perspiciatis unde omnis iste natus error sit voluptatem accusantium doloremque laudantium, totam rem aperiam, eaque ipsa quae ab illo inventore veritatis et quasi architecto beatae vitae dicta sunt explicabo. Nemo enim ipsam voluptatem quia voluptas sit aspernatur aut odit aut fugit, sed quia consequuntur magni dolores eos qui ratione voluptatem sequi nesciunt. Neque porro quisquam est, qui dolorem ipsum quia dolor sit amet, consectetur, adipisci velit, sed quia non numquam eius modi tempora incidunt ut labore et dolore magnam aliquam quaerat voluptatem. Ut enim ad minima veniam, quis nostrum exercitationem ullam corporis suscipit laboriosam, nisi ut aliquid ex ea commodi consequatur? Quis autem vel eum iure reprehenderit qui in ea voluptate velit esse quam nihil molestiae consequatur, vel illum qui dolorem eum fugiat quo voluptas nulla pariatur?"

1914 translation by H. Rackham

"But I must explain to you how all this mistaken idea of denouncing pleasure and praising pain was born and I will give you a complete account of the system, and expound the actual teachings of the great explorer of the truth, the master-builder of human happiness. No one rejects, dislikes, or avoids pleasure itself, because it is pleasure, but because those who do not know how to pursue pleasure rationally encounter consequences that are extremely painful. Nor again is there anyone who loves or pursues or desires to obtain pain of itself, because it is pain, but because occasionally circumstances occur in which toil and pain can procure him some great pleasure. To take a trivial example, which of us ever undertakes laborious physical exercise, except to obtain some advantage from it? But who has any right to find fault with a man who chooses to enjoy a pleasure that has no annoying consequences, or one who avoids a pain that produces no resultant pleasure?"

Section 1.10.33 of "de Finibus Bonorum et Malorum", written by Cicero in 45 BC

"At vero eos et accusamus et iusto odio dignissimos ducimus qui blanditiis praesentium voluptatum deleniti atque corrupti quos dolores et quas molestias excepturi sint occaecati cupiditate non provident, similique sunt in culpa qui officia deserunt mollitia animi, id est laborum et dolorum fuga. Et harum quidem rerum facilis est et expedita distinctio. Nam libero tempore, cum soluta nobis est eligendi optio cumque nihil impedit quo minus id quod maxime placeat facere possimus, omnis voluptas assumenda est, omnis dolor repellendus. Temporibus autem quibusdam et aut officiis debitis aut rerum necessitatibus saepe eveniet ut et voluptates repudiandae sint et molestiae non recusandae. Itaque earum rerum hic tenetur a sapiente delectus, ut aut reiciendis voluptatibus maiores alias consequatur aut perferendis doloribus asperiores repellat."

1914 translation by H. Rackham

"On the other hand, we denounce with righteous indignation and dislike men who are so beguiled and demoralized by the charms of pleasure of the moment, so blinded by desire, that they cannot foresee the pain and trouble that are bound to ensue; and equal blame belongs to those who fail in their duty through weakness of will, which is the same as saying through shrinking from toil and pain. These cases are perfectly simple and easy to distinguish. In a free hour, when our power of choice is untrammelled and when nothing prevents our being able to do what we like best, every pleasure is to be welcomed and every pain avoided. But in certain circumstances and owing to the claims of duty or the obligations of business it will frequently occur that pleasures have to be repudiated and annoyances accepted. The wise man therefore always holds in these matters to this principle of selection: he rejects pleasures to secure other greater pleasures, or else he endures pains to avoid worse pains."

What is Lorem Ipsum?

Lorem Ipsum is simply dummy text of the printing and typesetting industry. Lorem Ipsum has been the industry's standard dummy text ever since the 1500s, when an unknown printer took a galley of type and scrambled it to make a type specimen book. It has survived not only five centuries, but also the leap into electronic typesetting, remaining essentially unchanged. It was popularised in the 1960s with the release of Letraset sheets containing Lorem Ipsum passages, and more recently with desktop publishing software like Aldus PageMaker including versions of Lorem Ipsum.

Why do we use it?

It is a long established fact that a reader will be distracted by the readable content of a page when looking at its layout. The point of using Lorem Ipsum is that it has a more-or-less normal distribution of letters, as opposed to using 'Content here, content here', making it look like readable English. Many desktop publishing packages and web page editors now use Lorem Ipsum as their default model text, and a search for 'lorem ipsum' will uncover many web sites still in their infancy. Various versions have evolved over the years, sometimes by accident, sometimes on purpose (injected humour and the like).

Where does it come from?
Contrary to popular belief, Lorem Ipsum is not simply random text. It has roots in a piece of classical Latin literature from 45 BC, making it over 2000 years old. Richard McClintock, a Latin professor at Hampden-Sydney College in Virginia, looked up one of the more obscure Latin words, consectetur, from a Lorem Ipsum passage, and going through the cites of the word in classical literature, discovered the undoubtable source. Lorem Ipsum comes from sections 1.10.32 and 1.10.33 of "de Finibus Bonorum et Malorum" (The Extremes of Good and Evil) by Cicero, written in 45 BC. This book is a treatise on the theory of ethics, very popular during the Renaissance. The first line of Lorem Ipsum, "Lorem ipsum dolor sit amet..", comes from a line in section 1.10.32.

The standard chunk of Lorem Ipsum used since the 1500s is reproduced below for those interested. Sections 1.10.32 and 1.10.33 from "de Finibus Bonorum et Malorum" by Cicero are also reproduced in their exact original form, accompanied by English versions from the 1914 translation by H. Rackham.

Where can I get some?
There are many variations of passages of Lorem Ipsum available, but the majority have suffered alteration in some form, by injected humour, or randomised words which don't look even slightly believable. If you are going to use a passage of Lorem Ipsum, you need to be sure there isn't anything embarrassing hidden in the middle of text. All the Lorem Ipsum generators on the Internet tend to repeat predefined chunks as necessary, making this the first true generator on the Internet. It uses a dictionary of over 200 Latin words, combined with a handful of model sentence

structures, to generate Lorem Ipsum which looks reasonable. The generated Lorem Ipsum is therefore always free from repetition, injected humour, or non-characteristic words etc.

The standard Lorem Ipsum passage, used since the 1500s

"Lorem ipsum dolor sit amet, consectetur adipiscing elit, sed do eiusmod tempor incididunt ut labore et dolore magna aliqua. Ut enim ad minim veniam, quis nostrud exercitation ullamco laboris nisi ut aliquip ex ea commodo consequat. Duis aute irure dolor in reprehenderit in voluptate velit esse cillum dolore eu fugiat nulla pariatur. Excepteur sint occaecat cupidatat non proident, sunt in culpa qui officia deserunt mollit anim id est laborum."

Section 1.10.32 of "de Finibus Bonorum et Malorum", written by Cicero in 45 BC

"Sed ut perspiciatis unde omnis iste natus error sit voluptatem accusantium doloremque laudantium, totam rem aperiam, eaque ipsa quae ab illo inventore veritatis et quasi architecto beatae vitae dicta sunt explicabo. Nemo enim ipsam voluptatem quia voluptas sit aspernatur aut odit aut fugit, sed quia consequuntur magni dolores eos qui ratione voluptatem sequi nesciunt. Neque porro quisquam est, qui dolorem ipsum quia dolor sit amet, consectetur, adipisci velit, sed quia non numquam eius modi tempora incidunt ut labore et dolore magnam aliquam quaerat voluptatem. Ut enim ad minima veniam, quis nostrum exercitationem ullam corporis suscipit laboriosam, nisi ut aliquid ex ea commodi consequatur? Quis autem vel eum iure reprehenderit qui in ea voluptate velit esse quam nihil molestiae consequatur, vel illum qui dolorem eum fugiat quo voluptas nulla pariatur?"

1914 translation by H. Rackham

"But I must explain to you how all this mistaken idea of denouncing pleasure and praising pain was born and I will give you a complete account of the system, and expound the actual teachings of the great explorer of the truth, the master-builder of human happiness. No one rejects, dislikes, or avoids pleasure itself, because it is pleasure, but because those who do not know how to pursue pleasure rationally encounter consequences that are extremely painful. Nor again is there anyone who loves or pursues or desires to obtain pain of itself, because it is pain, but because occasionally circumstances occur in which toil and pain can procure him some great pleasure. To take a trivial example, which of us ever undertakes laborious physical exercise, except to obtain some advantage from it? But who has any right to find fault with a man who chooses to enjoy a pleasure that has no annoying consequences, or one who avoids a pain that produces no resultant pleasure?"

Section 1.10.33 of "de Finibus Bonorum et Malorum", written by Cicero in 45 BC

"At vero eos et accusamus et iusto odio dignissimos ducimus qui blanditiis praesentium voluptatum deleniti atque corrupti quos dolores et quas molestias excepturi sint occaecati cupiditate non provident, similique sunt in culpa qui officia deserunt mollitia animi, id est laborum et dolorum fuga. Et harum quidem rerum facilis est et expedita distinctio. Nam libero tempore, cum soluta nobis est eligendi optio cumque nihil impedit quo minus id quod maxime placeat facere possimus, omnis voluptas assumenda est, omnis dolor repellendus. Temporibus autem quibusdam et aut officiis debitis aut rerum necessitatibus saepe eveniet ut et voluptates repudiandae sint et molestiae non recusandae. Itaque earum rerum hic

tenetur a sapiente delectus, ut aut reiciendis voluptatibus maiores alias consequatur aut perferendis doloribus asperiores repellat."

1914 translation by H. Rackham

"On the other hand, we denounce with righteous indignation and dislike men who are so beguiled and demoralized by the charms of pleasure of the moment, so blinded by desire, that they cannot foresee the pain and trouble that are bound to ensue; and equal blame belongs to those who fail in their duty through weakness of will, which is the same as saying through shrinking from toil and pain. These cases are perfectly simple and easy to distinguish. In a free hour, when our power of choice is untrammelled and when nothing prevents our being able to do what we like best, every pleasure is to be welcomed and every pain avoided. But in certain circumstances and owing to the claims of duty or the obligations of business it will frequently occur that pleasures have to be repudiated and annoyances accepted. The wise man therefore always holds in these matters to this principle of selection: he rejects pleasures to secure other greater pleasures, or else he endures pains to avoid worse pains."

What is Lorem Ipsum?

Lorem Ipsum is simply dummy text of the printing and typesetting industry. Lorem Ipsum has been the industry's standard dummy text ever since the 1500s, when an unknown printer took a galley of type and scrambled it to make a type specimen book. It has survived not only five centuries, but also the leap into electronic typesetting, remaining essentially unchanged. It was popularised in the 1960s with the release of Letraset sheets containing Lorem Ipsum passages, and more recently with desktop publishing software like Aldus PageMaker including versions of Lorem

Ipsum.

Why do we use it?

It is a long established fact that a reader will be distracted by the readable content of a page when looking at its layout. The point of using Lorem Ipsum is that it has a more-or-less normal distribution of letters, as opposed to using 'Content here, content here', making it look like readable English. Many desktop publishing packages and web page editors now use Lorem Ipsum as their default model text, and a search for 'lorem ipsum' will uncover many web sites still in their infancy. Various versions have evolved over the years, sometimes by accident, sometimes on purpose (injected humour and the like).

Where does it come from?

Contrary to popular belief, Lorem Ipsum is not simply random text. It has roots in a piece of classical Latin literature from 45 BC, making it over 2000 years old. Richard McClintock, a Latin professor at Hampden-Sydney College in Virginia, looked up one of the more obscure Latin words, consectetur, from a Lorem Ipsum passage, and going through the cites of the word in classical literature, discovered the undoubtable source. Lorem Ipsum comes from sections 1.10.32 and 1.10.33 of "de Finibus Bonorum et Malorum" (The Extremes of Good and Evil) by Cicero, written in 45 BC. This book is a treatise on the theory of ethics, very popular during the Renaissance. The first line of Lorem Ipsum, "Lorem ipsum dolor sit amet..", comes from a line in section 1.10.32.

The standard chunk of Lorem Ipsum used since the 1500s is reproduced below for those interested. Sections 1.10.32 and 1.10.33 from "de Finibus Bonorum et Malorum" by Cicero are also reproduced in their exact

original form, accompanied by English versions from the 1914 translation by H. Rackham.

Where can I get some?

There are many variations of passages of Lorem Ipsum available, but the majority have suffered alteration in some form, by injected humour, or randomised words which don't look even slightly believable. If you are going to use a passage of Lorem Ipsum, you need to be sure there isn't anything embarrassing hidden in the middle of text. All the Lorem Ipsum generators on the Internet tend to repeat predefined chunks as necessary, making this the first true generator on the Internet. It uses a dictionary of over 200 Latin words, combined with a handful of model sentence structures, to generate Lorem Ipsum which looks reasonable. The generated Lorem Ipsum is therefore always free from repetition, injected humour, or non-characteristic words etc.

The standard Lorem Ipsum passage, used since the 1500s

"Lorem ipsum dolor sit amet, consectetur adipiscing elit, sed do eiusmod tempor incididunt ut labore et dolore magna aliqua. Ut enim ad minim veniam, quis nostrud exercitation ullamco laboris nisi ut aliquip ex ea commodo consequat. Duis aute irure dolor in reprehenderit in voluptate velit esse cillum dolore eu fugiat nulla pariatur. Excepteur sint occaecat cupidatat non proident, sunt in culpa qui officia deserunt mollit anim id est laborum."

Section 1.10.32 of "de Finibus Bonorum et Malorum", written by Cicero in 45 BC

"Sed ut perspiciatis unde omnis iste natus error sit voluptatem accusantium doloremque laudantium, totam rem aperiam, eaque ipsa quae ab illo inventore veritatis et quasi architecto beatae vitae dicta sunt explicabo. Nemo

enim ipsam voluptatem quia voluptas sit aspernatur aut odit aut fugit, sed quia consequuntur magni dolores eos qui ratione voluptatem sequi nesciunt. Neque porro quisquam est, qui dolorem ipsum quia dolor sit amet, consectetur, adipisci velit, sed quia non numquam eius modi tempora incidunt ut labore et dolore magnam aliquam quaerat voluptatem. Ut enim ad minima veniam, quis nostrum exercitationem ullam corporis suscipit laboriosam, nisi ut aliquid ex ea commodi consequatur? Quis autem vel eum iure reprehenderit qui in ea voluptate velit esse quam nihil molestiae consequatur, vel illum qui dolorem eum fugiat quo voluptas nulla pariatur?"

1914 translation by H. Rackham

"But I must explain to you how all this mistaken idea of denouncing pleasure and praising pain was born and I will give you a complete account of the system, and expound the actual teachings of the great explorer of the truth, the master-builder of human happiness. No one rejects, dislikes, or avoids pleasure itself, because it is pleasure, but because those who do not know how to pursue pleasure rationally encounter consequences that are extremely painful. Nor again is there anyone who loves or pursues or desires to obtain pain of itself, because it is pain, but because occasionally circumstances occur in which toil and pain can procure him some great pleasure. To take a trivial example, which of us ever undertakes laborious physical exercise, except to obtain some advantage from it? But who has any right to find fault with a man who chooses to enjoy a pleasure that has no annoying consequences, or one who avoids a pain that produces no resultant pleasure?"

Section 1.10.33 of "de Finibus Bonorum et Malorum", written by Cicero in 45 BC

"At vero eos et accusamus et iusto odio dignissimos

ducimus qui blanditiis praesentium voluptatum deleniti atque corrupti quos dolores et quas molestias excepturi sint occaecati cupiditate non provident, similique sunt in culpa qui officia deserunt mollitia animi, id est laborum et dolorum fuga. Et harum quidem rerum facilis est et expedita distinctio. Nam libero tempore, cum soluta nobis est eligendi optio cumque nihil impedit quo minus id quod maxime placeat facere possimus, omnis voluptas assumenda est, omnis dolor repellendus. Temporibus autem quibusdam et aut officiis debitis aut rerum necessitatibus saepe eveniet ut et voluptates repudiandae sint et molestiae non recusandae. Itaque earum rerum hic tenetur a sapiente delectus, ut aut reiciendis voluptatibus maiores alias consequatur aut perferendis doloribus asperiores repellat."

1914 translation by H. Rackham

"On the other hand, we denounce with righteous indignation and dislike men who are so beguiled and demoralized by the charms of pleasure of the moment, so blinded by desire, that they cannot foresee the pain and trouble that are bound to ensue; and equal blame belongs to those who fail in their duty through weakness of will, which is the same as saying through shrinking from toil and pain. These cases are perfectly simple and easy to distinguish. In a free hour, when our power of choice is untrammelled and when nothing prevents our being able to do what we like best, every pleasure is to be welcomed and every pain avoided. But in certain circumstances and owing to the claims of duty or the obligations of business it will frequently occur that pleasures have to be repudiated and annoyances accepted. The wise man therefore always holds in these matters to this principle of selection: he rejects pleasures to secure other greater pleasures, or else

he endures pains to avoid worse pains."